United States
Social Studies
Engaging Cooperative Learning Activities

Stefanie McKoy

Kagan

Kagan Publishing
981 Calle Amanecer
San Clemente, CA 92673
1 (800) 933-2667
www.KaganOnline.com

ISBN: 978-1-933445-41-0

U.S. Social Studies

Featured Topics

United States Social Studies: Engaging Cooperative Learning Activities
Kagan Publishing • 800.933.2667 • www.KaganOnline.com

3

U.S. Social Studies
Table of Contents

United States Social Studies: Engaging Cooperative Learning Activities
Kagan Publishing • 800.933.2667 • www.KaganOnline.com

Table of Activities

United States Social Studies: Engaging Cooperative Learning Activities
Kagan Publishing • 800.933.2667 • www.KaganOnline.com

5

Historic Documents Activities

Formation of a New Government Activities

Westward Expansion Activities

6

United States Social Studies: Engaging Cooperative Learning Activities
Kagan Publishing • 800.933.2667 • www.KaganOnline.com

The Civil War and Reconstruction Activities

Industrialization Activities

United States Social Studies: Engaging Cooperative Learning Activities
Kagan Publishing • 800.933.2667 • www.KaganOnline.com

7

World War I Activities

The Great Depression Activities

World War II Activities

National Symbols Activities

United States Social Studies: Engaging Cooperative Learning Activities
Kagan Publishing • 800.933.2667 • www.KaganOnline.com

9

Introduction

Dear Educators,

First, I want to thank you for picking up this resource to use with your class. As a current educator myself, I strive to provide great resources that can enrich any social studies classroom.

This project began over 10 years ago as I began to use Kagan Structures in my classroom after attending a week-long institute after just completing my first year of teaching. I wanted to find a way to motivate and engage students in my classroom. I instantly fell in love with the Kagan Structures because it made it easy for me to infuse engaging cooperative learning into the content I am required to teach.

I found myself creating structure-based activities for the classroom and sharing them with other teachers who attended the same workshop and who also love to incorporate the structures into the classroom. Thus I began writing resources for Kagan Publishing, and this book marks my seventh book! I found myself creating numerous social studies activities to use in my classroom after switching grade levels. As a result, *United States Social Studies: Engaging Cooperative Learning Activities* was born!

The activities are based on ten Kagan Structures: Fan-N-Pick, Find Someone Who, Mix-N-Match, Mix-Pair-Share, Quiz-Quiz-Trade, RallyCoach, Sage-N-Scribe, Showdown, Think-Write-RoundRobin, and Who Am I?. These structures incorporate pair work, teamwork, and whole-class interactions. Each structure is highly interactive and encourages teamwork among students to learn and understand United States history. History can be a tricky subject for students and students love that cooperative learning allows for developing a deeper understanding.

This book could not have been possible without the support of my fifth-grade students at Cedar Ridge Intermediate in Branson, Missouri, because they tested, critiqued, and offered suggestions for each activity presented in the book. The process of writing a book, even a resource for teachers, is a valuable skill I was able to give to my students through this great opportunity given to me.

I also need to thank my fellow fifth-grade team because they were very enthusiastic to try activities in the classroom and allowed me to ask numerous questions about what they would like to see. I also want to thank my administrators for continuing to support my "crazy" ideas and offering encouragement through the book publishing process.

I need to thank my good friend, Laura Eakins with PhotoBox Studio, for taking my picture and keeping my son entertained while I worked on this project. My family also deserves a huge thank you for being my biggest cheerleaders! I couldn't do it without the love of my husband, Clint, and the hugs from my son, Kolby!

Finally, I must thank those at Kagan for working with me on another project and trusting me with this responsibility. Appreciation goes to Miguel Kagan for his guidance and review of my manuscript; Alex Core for making the book come alive with his design and cover color; Becky Herrington for managing the publication; Erin Kant for illustrations; and Ginny Harvey for copyediting.

Happy teaching!

Stefanie McKoy

Stefanie McKoy,
Educator

About the Author

Stefanie McKoy graduated from Missouri State University in Springfield, Missouri, with a Bachelor of Arts degree in Elementary Education and holds a Master of Arts in Educational Technology Leadership from the University of Arkansas in Fayetteville, Arkansas. She is currently certified in both Early Childhood and Elementary Education in addition to her eMINTS certification. Stefanie is currently teaching fifth grade in the Branson School District. Stefanie resides in Ozark, Missouri, with her husband and young son. She enjoys reading, teaching swimming lessons, spending time boating with her in-laws and visiting antique shops with her mother, who is also her best friend.

10

United States Social Studies: Engaging Cooperative Learning Activities
Kagan Publishing • 800.933.2667 • www.KaganOnline.com

Structures

Fan-N-Pick

Teammates play a card game to respond to questions. Roles rotate with each new question.

Setup: *Each team receives a set of question or problem cards.*

1 Student #1 Fans Cards

Student #1 holds question cards in a fan and says, *"Pick a card, any card!"*

2 Student #2 Picks a Card

Student #2 picks a card, reads the question aloud to the team, holds the card up so Student #3 can see the question for 5 seconds, and then lays the card down. (For cards that have answers on the back, Student #2 passes the card to Student #4 to check for correctness.) *"What branch of government is responsible for making laws?"*

3 Student #3 Answers

Student #3 answers the question. *"It's the Legislative branch."* For higher-level thinking questions, students share elaborated answers.

United States Social Studies: Engaging Cooperative Learning Activities
Kagan Publishing • 800.933.2667 • www.KaganOnline.com

4 Student #4 Responds

Student #4 responds to the answer.

- For right or wrong answers: Student #4 checks the answer and then either praises or tutors the student who answered. *"That's correct! You're a true genius."* or *"I don't think that's correct; let's look it up together."*

- For higher-level thinking questions that have no right or wrong answer: Student #4 does not check for correctness, but praises the thinking that went into the answer and/or paraphrases. *"You gave several facts about what Thomas "Stonewall" Jackson was known for. I like the way you approached the question."*

5 Rotate Roles

Teammates rotate roles, one person clockwise for each new round.

Modifications

Fan-N-Pick can be played in pairs. Student #1 fans; Student #2 picks and reads; Student #1 answers; Student #2 tutors or praises; students switch roles.

Fan-N-Pick Activities

United States Social Studies: Engaging Cooperative Learning Activities
Kagan Publishing • 800.933.2667 • www.KaganOnline.com

13

Find Someone Who

Students circulate through the classroom, forming and re-forming pairs, trying to "find someone who" knows an answer, and then they become "someone who knows."

Setup: The teacher prepares a worksheet or questions for students.

1 Students Mix

With worksheets in one hand and the other hand raised, students circulate through the room until they find a partner. *"Mix in the room and pair up with a student with a hand up. Put your hands down, and then each partner asks the other one question from the worksheet. If your partner knows an answer, write the answer in your own words, and then have your partner sign your sheet to show agreement."*

2 Partner A Asks a Question

In pairs, Partner A asks a question from the worksheet; Partner B answers. Partner A records the answer on his or her own worksheet.

3 Partner B Checks

Partner B checks the answer and initials it, indicating agreement.

4 Partner B Asks a Question

Partner B now asks a question; Partner A responds. Partner B records the answer on his or her own worksheet.

5 Partner A Checks

Partner A checks the answer and initials it, indicating agreement.

6 Partners Depart

Partners shake hands, part, and raise a hand again as they search for a new partner.

United States Social Studies: Engaging Cooperative Learning Activities
Kagan Publishing • 800.933.2667 • www.KaganOnline.com

7 Continue Finding Someone Who

Students continue mixing and pairing until their worksheets are complete.

8 Students Sit

When their worksheets are completed, students sit down; seated students may be approached by others as a resource. Alternatively, finished students may stand along a wall or on the outside perimeter of the room.

9 Teams Compare Answers

When all students are done, or the teacher calls time, students return to their teams to compare answers; in the case of disagreement or uncertainty, they can consult a neighbor team or raise four hands to ask a team question. *"Please return to your team and then RoundRobin read the question and share the answer. If you have different answers, work it out in your team. If you can't agree, get help from a nearby team, or raise four hands to ask a team question."*

Find Someone Who Activities

United States Social Studies: Engaging Cooperative Learning Activities
Kagan Publishing • 800.933.2667 • www.KaganOnline.com

15

Mix-N-Match

*Students mix, repeatedly quizzing new partners and trading cards.
Afterwards, they rush to find a partner with the card that matches theirs.*

Setup: *The teacher provides or students create pairs of matching cards.*

1 Students Mix and Pair

With a card in one hand and the other hand raised, each student mixes around the room, looking for a partner with a raised hand. When they pair up, they give each other a high five. *"Pair up with another student with a raised hand. Give each other a high five, and then lower your hands."*

Robert E. Lee

General of the Confederate Army

2 Partner A Asks a Question

In the pair, Partner A asks Partner B a question from his or her card. For example Partner A's card says, *"What does the First Amendment state?"*

3 Partner B Answers

Partner B answers Partner A's question. *"Freedom of speech, religion, press..."*

4 Partner A Praises or Coaches

If Partner B answers correctly, Partner A provides praise. *"Right! You rock at the Bill of Rights!"* If Partner B answers incorrectly, Partner A provides the correct answer and coaches or tutors Partner B. *"Not quite! It's about personal freedoms..."*

5 Partners Switch Roles

Partners switch roles. Partner B now asks the question and offers praise or coaching.

16

United States Social Studies: Engaging Cooperative Learning Activities
Kagan Publishing • 800.933.2667 • www.KaganOnline.com

6 Partners Trade Cards

Before departing and looking for new partners, partners trade cards.

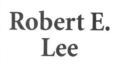

Robert E. Lee

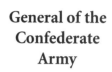

General of the Confederate Army

7 Continue Quizzing and Trading

Partners split up and continue quizzing and getting quizzed by new partners. When done, they trade cards again and find a new partner.

8 Teacher Calls "Freeze"

After a sufficient time of quizzing and trading cards, the teacher calls "*Freeze.*" Students freeze, hide their cards, and think of their match.

9 Find Match

The teacher calls "*Match.*" Students search for a classmate with the matching card. For example, the student with the First Amendment card pairs up with the student with the card that says, "Freedom of Speech…" When they find each other, they move to the outside of the classroom and stand shoulder to shoulder. This way, students still searching for a match can find each other more easily.

10 Teacher Checks Answer

The teacher selects a pair to begin. The pair shares their answer by stating what they have on their own cards. Alternatively, the teacher has students hold up their cards and does a quick visual answer check.

Mix-N-Match Activities

United States Social Studies: Engaging Cooperative Learning Activities
Kagan Publishing • 800.933.2667 • www.KaganOnline.com

17

Mix-Pair-Share

The class "mixes" until the teacher calls, "pair." Students find a new partner to discuss or answer the teacher's question.

Setup: The teacher prepares questions to ask students.

1 Students Mix

Students mix around the room.

2 Students Pair

Teacher calls *"Pair."*

3 Students Find a Partner

Students pair up with the person closest to them and give a high five. Students who haven't found a partner raise their hands to find each other.

4 Teacher Asks a Question

Teacher asks a question and gives Think Time.

United States Social Studies: Engaging Cooperative Learning Activities
Kagan Publishing • 800.933.2667 • www.KaganOnline.com

5 Students Share

Students share with their partners using:
- Timed Pair Share
- RallyRobin

Optional

Students may practice greetings or affirmations during Step 1.

Hint

For oral lists (name U.S. military leaders during WWII), use RallyRobin. For longer, in-depth responses (what role did these leaders play), use Timed Pair Share.

Mix-Pair-Share Activities

United States Social Studies: Engaging Cooperative Learning Activities
Kagan Publishing • 800.933.2667 • www.KaganOnline.com

19

Quiz-Quiz-Trade

Students quiz a partner, get quizzed by a partner, and then trade cards to repeat the process with a new partner.

Setup: *The teacher prepares a set of question cards for the class, or each student creates a question card.*

1 Students Pair Up

With a card in one hand and the other hand raised, each student stands up, puts a hand up, and pairs up with a classmate. They give each other a high five as they pair up. *"Alright everyone, stand up, hand up, pair up. High five when you pair up and lower your hands so everyone can quickly find a partner with a hand up."*

2 Partner A Quizzes

In the pair, Partner A asks Partner B a question relating to his or her card. For example, *"My card says: Which two groups fought during the Civil War?"*

3 Partner B Answers

Partner B answers Partner A's question. *"The North and the South, the Union and the Confederate."*

4 Partner A Praises or Coaches

If Partner B answers correctly, Partner A praises him or her. If Partner B answers incorrectly, Partner A coaches or tutors Partner B.

United States Social Studies: Engaging Cooperative Learning Activities
Kagan Publishing • 800.933.2667 • www.KaganOnline.com

5 Switch Roles

Partners switch roles. Partner B now asks the question on his or her card and offers praise or coaches.

6 Partners Trade Cards

Before departing and looking for new partners, partners trade cards. This way, students have a new card for each new pairing.

7 Partners Continue Quizzing and Trading

Partners split up and continue quizzing and getting quizzed by new partners. When done, they trade cards again and find a new partner. Remind students, "*Put a hand up to find a partner, and hands down when you have a partner.*"

Quiz-Quiz-Trade Activities

United States Social Studies: *Engaging Cooperative Learning Activities*
Kagan Publishing • 800.933.2667 • www.KaganOnline.com

21

RallyCoach

Partners take turns, one solving a problem while the other coaches.

Setup: Each pair needs one set of questions and one pencil.

1 Partner A Solves

In shoulder partners, Partner A solves the first problem, saying the steps or procedures aloud.

2 Partner B Coaches and Praises

Partner B acts as the coach. Partner B watches, listens, and checks. If Partner A gets an incorrect answer or needs help, Partner B coaches. If Partner A solves the problem correctly, Partner B praises.

3 Partner B Solves

Students switch roles and Partner B now solves the next problem, talking it out.

22

United States Social Studies: Engaging Cooperative Learning Activities
Kagan Publishing • 800.933.2667 • www.KaganOnline.com

4 Partner A Coaches and Praises

Partner A now acts as the coach: watching, listening, checking, coaching, and praising.

5 Continue Solving

The process is repeated for each new problem.

Note

RallyCoach may be used with worksheet problems, oral problems provided by the teacher, or problems posted or projected for the class.

Variation

Pairs Check. After solving two problems, pairs check their answers with the other pair in their team.

RallyCoach Activities

United States Social Studies: Engaging Cooperative Learning Activities
Kagan Publishing • 800.933.2667 • www.KaganOnline.com

23

Sage-N-Scribe

Partners take turns being the Sage and the Scribe.

Setup: *In pairs, Student A is the Sage; Student B is the Scribe. Students fold a sheet of paper in half and each writes his or her name on one half.*

1 Sage Instructs Scribe

The Sage orally describes to the Scribe how to perform a task or solve a problem. For example, the Sage's instruction to the Scribe on how to remember the first words of the Constitution is to think, *"It was written for us, we the people."*

2 Scribe Writes Solution, Tutors if Necessary

The Scribe solves the problem in writing according to the Sage's step-by-step oral instructions. If the Sage gives incorrect instructions, the Scribe tutors the Sage. *"I think the instructions need more clarity. Let's discuss further."*

24

United States Social Studies: Engaging Cooperative Learning Activities
Kagan Publishing • 800.933.2667 • www.KaganOnline.com

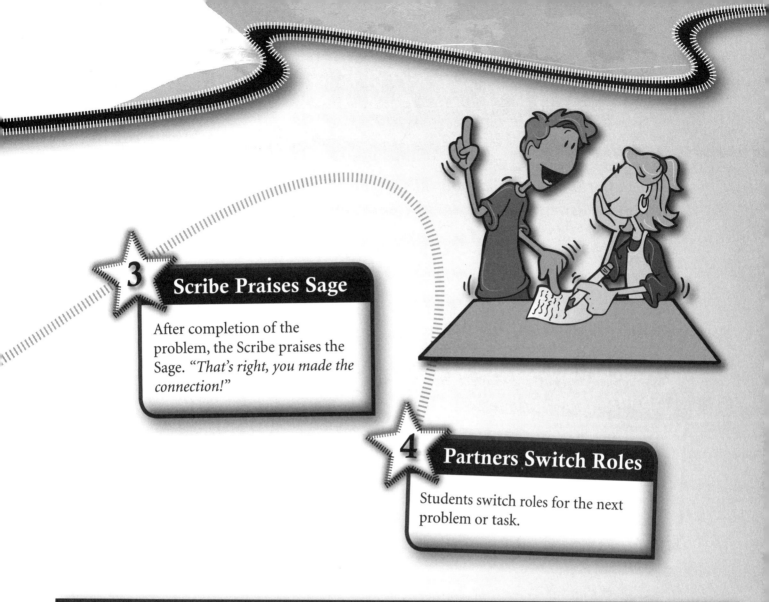

3 Scribe Praises Sage

After completion of the problem, the Scribe praises the Sage. *"That's right, you made the connection!"*

4 Partners Switch Roles

Students switch roles for the next problem or task.

Sage-N-Scribe Activities

United States Social Studies: Engaging Cooperative Learning Activities
Kagan Publishing • 800.933.2667 • www.KaganOnline.com

25

Showdown

When the Showdown Captain calls, "Showdown!" teammates all display their own answers. Teammates either celebrate or tutor, and then celebrate.

Setup: *The teacher prepares a set of questions or problems. Questions may be provided to each team as question cards that they stack face-down in the cent of the table. Each student has a slate or response board and a writing utensil.*

1 Teacher Selects the Showdown Captain

The teacher selects one student on each team to be the Showdown Captain for the first round. "*Student #4 is the first Showdown Captain. Rotate the role clockwise after each question.*"

2 Showdown Captain Reads a Question

The Showdown Captain reads the first question. If using question cards, the Showdown Captain draws the top card, reads the question, shows it to the team, and provides Think Time. "*Think about your answer.*"

3 Students Answer Independently

Working alone, all students write their answers and keep their answers to themselves, hidden from teammates.

4 Teammates Signal When Done

When finished, teammates signal they're ready by turning over their response boards, putting down their markers, or giving a hand signal.

5 Showdown Captain Calls "Showdown"

The Showdown Captain calls "*Showdown!*"

26

United States Social Studies: Engaging Cooperative Learning Activities
Kagan Publishing • 800.933.2667 • www.KaganOnline.com

6 Teams Show Their Answers

Teammates simultaneously show their answers and RoundRobin state them in turn.

7 Teams Check for Accuracy

The Showdown Captain leads the team in checking for accuracy. *"Great. We all got the same answer."*

8 Celebrate or Coach

If all teammates have the correct answer, the Showdown Captain leads the team in a celebration. If a teammate has an incorrect answer, teammates coach the student or students with the incorrect answer, and then celebrate.

9 Rotate the Showdown Captain Role

The person on the left of the Showdown Captain becomes the Showdown Captain for the next round.

Showdown Activities

United States Social Studies: Engaging Cooperative Learning Activities
Kagan Publishing • 800.933.2667 • www.KaganOnline.com

27

Think-Write-RoundRobin

Students take turns sharing their writing with teammates.

Setup: *The teacher prepares a set of questions or a writing assignment. Each teammate receives a pen or pencil and piece of paper to record his or her response or responses.*

1 Teacher Asks a Question

The teacher presents a question or assigns a writing (or drawing) task. For example, *"What caused the Great Depression? Describe possible causes."*

2 Think Time

The teacher provides students a silent 3 seconds of Think Time to think of their responses. *"Everyone think about what you can write."*

United States Social Studies: Engaging Cooperative Learning Activities
Kagan Publishing • 800.933.2667 • www.KaganOnline.com

Think-Write-RoundRobin Activities

3 Students Write

Students independently write (or draw) their responses. *"Write your own answer. No talking. Pencils down when you're done to signal you're ready for the RoundRobin."*

4 Teammates Take Turns Sharing

Students share their writing with their teammates, using RoundRobin.

United States Social Studies: Engaging Cooperative Learning Activities
Kagan Publishing • 800.933.2667 • www.KaganOnline.com

29

Who Am I?

Students attempt to discover a secret identity placed on their back.

Setup: *Teacher or students make cards with the name of historic characters or events. Without the student seeing the name of the character or event, the card is placed on the student's back.*

1 Students Pair Up

Students stand up and raise a hand until they find a partner. The pair gives a high five and then lowers their hands. *"Find a classmate with a hand up. Give each other a high five and then lower your hands."*

Patrick Henry

League of Nations

2 Partner A Asks Three Questions

Partner A turns around to show Partner B the card on his or her back. Partner A asks Partner B three yes-or-no questions to discover the secret identity. Questions might be: *"(1) Am I a person? (2) Am I male? (3) Am I a child?"* Partner B answers *"yes"* or *"no"* to each question.

United States Social Studies: Engaging Cooperative Learning Activities
Kagan Publishing • 800.933.2667 • www.KaganOnline.com

3 Partner B Asks Three Questions

Reverse roles. Partner B now asks three questions and Partner A answers.

4 Students Form New Partners and Continue

Partners shake hands, thank each other, and raise their hands to find a new partner.

Note

When it's their turn, students may make one guess at their identity with each partner. If they are wrong, they keep playing. If they are right, they move their identity card to their front, and become a helper, whispering clues to classmates.

Who Am I? Activities

United States Social Studies: Engaging Cooperative Learning Activities
Kagan Publishing • 800.933.2667 • www.KaganOnline.com

31

U.S. *Social Studies Activities*

American Indians

Cooperative Learning Activities

American Indians
Geographical Influences

Directions: Think about the prompt, and then write your own response. When done, RoundRobin share your writing with your teammates. Use the space at the bottom to record ideas your teammates share.

Prompt: How did the geographical locations determine the lifestyles of the American Indians? Use multiple examples from various tribal locations in your explanation.

My writing: _____

_____

_____

_____

_____

_____

_____

_____

_____

_____

Ideas Teammates Share

United States Social Studies: Engaging Cooperative Learning Activities
Kagan Publishing • 800.933.2667 • www.KaganOnline.com

American Indians
Iroquois

■ **RallyCoach Directions:** Take turns answering each question as your partner coaches. Explain your thinking to your coach.
■ **Sage-N-Scribe Directions:** The Sage describes what he or she knows about the question so the Scribe can answer the question. The Sage and Scribe switch roles for each question.

Name _____

1. Which of the following were NOT a tribe that belonged to the Iroquois League?
   a) Pawnee
   b) Onondaga
   c) Tuscarora
   d) Mohawk

2. What food did the Iroquois people depend on?
   a) Sheep; grew crops such as corn and beans
   b) Buffalo
   c) Salmon, seal, bison
   d) Deer, bear, beaver, elk

3. Which sentence is true of the Iroquois people?
   a) They built canoes of birch bark.
   b) They grew crops such as corn and squash.
   c) They traveled throughout the land following food sources.
   d) Women tanned the hides of deer for clothing.

4. What do the Iroquois people call themselves?
   a) Wampanoag
   b) Algonquian
   c) Iroquois
   d) Haudenosaunee

Name _____

1. Where were the Iroquois located?
   a) Southwest Desert Cultural Region
   b) Great Plains Cultural Region
   c) Eastern Woodlands Cultural Region
   d) Northwest Coast Cultural Region

2. What type of housing did the Iroquois use?
   a) Tepee
   b) Longhouse
   c) Adobe
   d) Lodges

3. Which of the following was a symbol of the Iroquois people?
   a) Totem pole
   b) Wampum
   c) Tepees
   d) Tribal mask

4. Which sentence is true about the organization of the Iroquois League?
   a) Only tribal elders were allowed to participate.
   b) Tribes sent male representatives to the Great Council to make decisions for the league.
   c) Women did not have any influence in choosing the tribal representatives.
   d) Tribes sent two representatives to the Great Council meetings.

United States Social Studies: Engaging Cooperative Learning Activities
Kagan Publishing • 800.933.2667 • www.KaganOnline.com

37

American Indians
Northwest Coast Cultural Region

■ **RallyCoach Directions:** Take turns answering each question as your partner coaches. Explain your thinking to your coach.
■ **Sage-N-Scribe Directions:** The Sage describes what he or she knows about the question so the Scribe can answer the question. The Sage and Scribe switch roles for each question.

Name _____

1. Which of the following were NOT a tribe that belonged to the Northwest Coast cultural region?
   a) Inuit
   b) Kwakiutl
   c) Haida
   d) Tlingit

2. What natural resource did the tribes of the Northwest Coast cultural region depend on?
   a) Large mountain ranges
   b) Cedar trees
   c) Fertile fields
   d) Caves

3. What was the role of a shaman in the Northwest Coast cultural region?
   a) Help heal people who were ill
   b) Provide spiritual guidance in hard times
   c) Lead the tribe as a wise male elder
   d) Communicate with neighboring tribal communities

4. Which sentence best describes the housing of the Northwest Coast cultural region?
   a) Homes were built into the earth along the coast.
   b) Homes were built of sturdy planks and logs from the cedar trees.
   c) Homes were often small but housed many families.
   d) Homes were built of material that was easy to travel with during hunting season.

Name _____

1. What modern state contains a location of the Northwest Coast cultural region?
   a) Indiana
   b) Idaho
   c) Oregon
   d) California

2. What is a symbol popular to the Northwest Coast cultural region?
   a) Kachina dolls
   b) Birch tree canoes
   c) Clay pots
   d) Totem poles

3. Which of the following was NOT something hunted at sea in a dugout canoe?
   a) Whales
   b) Seals
   c) Sea otters
   d) Sharks

4. What tradition included ways to demonstrate wealth and involved gift giving?
   a) Potluck ceremony
   b) Potlatches
   c) Kwakiutl naming
   d) Elder council meetings

United States Social Studies: Engaging Cooperative Learning Activities
Kagan Publishing • 800.933.2667 • www.KaganOnline.com

American Indians
Plains Indians

Directions: Copy one set of cards for each team. Cut out each card along the dotted lines. Give each team a set of cards to play Fan-N-Pick or Showdown.

---

1 *American Indians*

What tribes were a part of the Great Plains cultural region?

Fan-N-Pick/Showdown

---

2 *American Indians*

What is geographically unique to the Great Plains region and shaped the lifestyle of the Plains Indians?

Fan-N-Pick/Showdown

---

3 *American Indians*

What animal was central to the way of life for the Great Plains Indians?

Fan-N-Pick/Showdown

---

4 *American Indians*

Great Plains Indians built villages along rivers. What type of house was used in these villages?

Fan-N-Pick/Showdown

---

5 *American Indians*

While on the hunt, what type of housing was used?

Fan-N-Pick/Showdown

---

6 *American Indians*

What advantage did the Cheyenne people have for trade that aided in hunting buffalo?

Fan-N-Pick/Showdown

---

7 *American Indians*

Where did the Great Plains Indians first acquire horses?

Fan-N-Pick/Showdown

---

8 *American Indians*

In what modern state do many Cheyenne people reside today?

Fan-N-Pick/Showdown

---

9 *American Indians*

What types of crops did the Great Plains Indians grow?

Fan-N-Pick/Showdown

---

10 *American Indians*

What weapons did the Great Plains Indians use to hunt?

Fan-N-Pick/Showdown

United States Social Studies: Engaging Cooperative Learning Activities
Kagan Publishing • 800.933.2667 • www.KaganOnline.com

39

American Indians
Southwest Desert Cultural Region

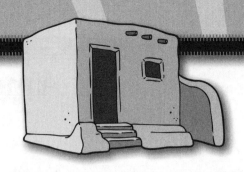

Name: _____

Directions: Pair up and take turns answering each question. Don't forget to get your partner's initials.

1

Name two tribes found in the Southwest Desert cultural region.

_____

_____

_____

_____

_____ **Initials**

2

What weather conditions describe the Southwest Desert cultural region?

_____

_____

_____

_____

_____ **Initials**

3

What did the Pueblo nation develop in order to grow crops such as corn, squash, and cotton?

_____

_____

_____

_____

_____ **Initials**

4

What was a role of the women in a Hopi tribe?

_____

_____

_____

_____

_____ **Initials**

5

What was the role of a man in a Hopi tribe?

_____

_____

_____

_____

_____ **Initials**

6

Name two characteristics of a Pueblo's housing.

_____

_____

_____

_____

_____ **Initials**

7

What is one tradition of the people of the Hopi tribe?

_____

_____

_____

_____

_____ **Initials**

8

Name two states where the Southwest Desert tribes could be found today?

_____

_____

_____

_____

_____ **Initials**

9

What was the purpose of the Kachina dolls?

_____

_____

_____

_____

_____ **Initials**

40

United States Social Studies: Engaging Cooperative Learning Activities
Kagan Publishing • 800.933.2667 • www.KaganOnline.com

American Indians
Dwellings

Directions: Cut out cards along the dotted lines. Distribute one card per student in sequence so for every student with a dwelling card, there is a student with a matching tribe card. Students use cards to play Mix-N-Match.

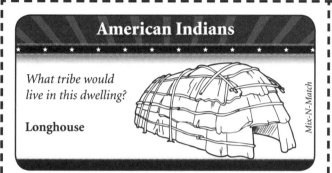

American Indians

What tribe would live in this dwelling?

Longhouse

Mix-N-Match

American Indians

Describe the dwelling this tribe would live in.

Iroquois

Mix-N-Match

American Indians

What tribe would live in this dwelling?

Lodge

Mix-N-Match

American Indians

Describe the dwelling this tribe would live in.

Great Plains Indians

Mix-N-Match

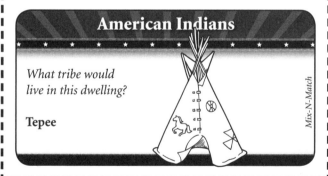

American Indians

What tribe would live in this dwelling?

Tepee

Mix-N-Match

American Indians

Describe the dwelling this tribe would live in.

Cheyenne

Mix-N-Match

American Indians

What tribe would live in this dwelling?

Adobe

Mix-N-Match

American Indians

Describe the dwelling this tribe would live in.

Hopi

Mix-N-Match

United States Social Studies: Engaging Cooperative Learning Activities
Kagan Publishing • 800.933.2667 • www.KaganOnline.com

41

American Indians
Dwellings

Directions: Cut out cards along the dotted lines. Distribute one card per student in sequence so for every student with a dwelling card, there is a student with a matching tribe card. Students use cards to play Mix-N-Match.

American Indians
What tribe would live in this dwelling?

Wigwam

Mix-N-Match

American Indians
Describe the dwelling this tribe would live in.
Algonquian Indians

Mix-N-Match

American Indians
What tribe would live in this dwelling?

Grass house

Mix-N-Match

American Indians
Describe the dwelling this tribe would live in.
Southern Plains Indians

Mix-N-Match

American Indians
What tribe would live in this dwelling?

Wattle and Daub house

Mix-N-Match

American Indians
Describe the dwelling this tribe would live in.
Southeastern Indians

Mix-N-Match

American Indians
What tribe would live in this dwelling?

Chickees

Mix-N-Match

American Indians
Describe the dwelling this tribe would live in.
Seminole Indians

Mix-N-Match

United States Social Studies: Engaging Cooperative Learning Activities
Kagan Publishing • 800.933.2667 • www.KaganOnline.com

American Indians
Dwellings

Directions: Cut out cards along the dotted lines. Distribute one card per student in sequence so for every student with a dwelling card, there is a student with a matching tribe card. Students use cards to play Mix-N-Match.

American Indians

What tribe would live in this dwelling?

Earthen house

Mix-N-Match

American Indians

Describe the dwelling this tribe would live in.

West Coast and Plateau Indians

Mix-N-Match

American Indians

What tribe would live in this dwelling?

Plank house

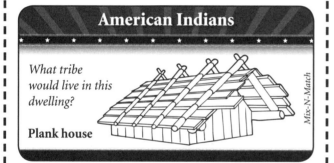

Mix-N-Match

American Indians

Describe the dwelling this tribe would live in.

Northwest Coast Indians

Mix-N-Match

American Indians

What tribe would live in this dwelling?

Igloo

Mix-N-Match

American Indians

Describe the dwelling this tribe would live in.

Inuit Indians

Mix-N-Match

United States Social Studies: Engaging Cooperative Learning Activities
Kagan Publishing • 800.933.2667 • www.KaganOnline.com

43

The American Colonies

The American Colonies

Life in the Colonies

Directions: Think about the prompt, and then write your own response. When done, RoundRobin share your writing with your teammates. Use the space at the bottom to record ideas your teammates share.

Prompt: Imagine you are a young apprentice living in an American colony in the 1700s. Write a detailed journal entry (including location) about a typical day in the life of an apprentice during the time of the American colonies.

My writing: _____

_____

_____

_____

_____

_____

_____

_____

_____

_____

Ideas Teammates Share

United States Social Studies: Engaging Cooperative Learning Activities
Kagan Publishing • 800.933.2667 • www.KaganOnline.com

The American Colonies
The 13 Colonies

■ **RallyCoach Directions:** Take turns answering each question as your partner coaches. Explain your thinking to your coach.
■ **Sage-N-Scribe Directions:** The Sage describes what he or she knows about the question so the Scribe can answer the question. The Sage and Scribe switch roles for each question.

Name _____

1. Which of the following is NOT a characteristic of the New England Colonies?
   a) Lived in small farms
   b) Traded fish, lumber, and furs
   c) Held a seaport in Salem and Boston
   d) Raised crops such as barley and rye

2. What commerce did the Middle Colonies use?
   a) Manufacturing of items such as leather goods
   b) Growing crops on plantations and owning slaves
   c) Trading fur along the Atlantic coast
   d) Exporting cotton groups

3. While many of the first colonies were founded for religious freedom, many held strict laws. What English colony was truly the first to offer freedom of religion?
   a) Massachusetts
   b) New England
   c) Rhode Island
   d) Salem

4. Why was the colony of Georgia founded?
   a) To give debtors from England a fresh start rather than place them in a crowded English jail
   b) To freely grow cotton on plantations with the use of slave labor
   c) To establish Quaker colonies in North America
   d) To offer a refuge for Catholics from English persecution

Name _____

1. Which of the following colonies was NOT part of the Middle Colonies?
   a) New York
   b) Virginia
   c) Delaware
   d) Maryland

2. Which group of colonies made a living primarily through farming such as tobacco and rice?
   a) New England
   b) Middle Colonies
   c) Southern Colonies
   d) Georgia

3. Who was the founder of the Connecticut colony, along with about one hundred followers?
   a) Thomas Hooker
   b) Anne Hutchinson
   c) Roger Williams
   d) William Penn

4. Geographically, what benefit did Georgia offer to the other colonies?
   a) A trade route through Georgia's vast rivers
   b) Protection from American Indian tribes due to the large mountain ranges
   c) Offered separation between the colonies and Spanish Florida
   d) The large, flat areas that offered protection from surprised European taxes

United States Social Studies: Engaging Cooperative Learning Activities
Kagan Publishing • 800.933.2667 • www.KaganOnline.com

47

The American Colonies
Colonial Times

Directions: Copy one set of cards for each team. Cut out each card along the dotted lines. Give each team a set of cards to play Fan-N-Pick or Showdown.

1 The American Colonies

How were merchants who formed the Virginia Company of London able to fund the settlement of Jamestown?

Fan-N-Pick/Showdown

2 The American Colonies

What caused the Jamestown Colony to be unsuccessful in the beginning?

Fan-N-Pick/Showdown

3 The American Colonies

Who eventually was elected leader of the Jamestown Colony and is known for his interaction with Pocahontas?

Fan-N-Pick/Showdown

4 The American Colonies

What crop native to America grew in popularity in England and other nations?

Fan-N-Pick/Showdown

5 The American Colonies

If a person from England wanted to travel to America and could not pay, what other choice was he or she offered?

Fan-N-Pick/Showdown

6 The American Colonies

What was the name of the law-making assembly in the English colonies?

Fan-N-Pick/Showdown

7 The American Colonies

When explorers came to North America, such as Samuel de Champlain, a French explorer, what were they searching for?

Fan-N-Pick/Showdown

8 The American Colonies

What were some reasons colonists came to the American colonies?

Fan-N-Pick/Showdown

United States Social Studies: Engaging Cooperative Learning Activities
Kagan Publishing • 800.933.2667 • www.KaganOnline.com

48

The American Colonies
Colonial Times

Directions: Copy one set of cards for each team. Cut out each card along the dotted lines. Give each team a set of cards to play Fan-N-Pick or Showdown.

---

9 *The American Colonies*

What is a pilgrim?

Fan-N-Pick/Showdown

---

10 *The American Colonies*

What led William Bradford and other Separatists to leave England?

Fan-N-Pick/Showdown

---

11 *The American Colonies*

What was the name of the Pilgrims of Plymouth written plan for their government?

Fan-N-Pick/Showdown

---

12 *The American Colonies*

Why was the first celebration of Thanksgiving held among the Pilgrims and the Wampanoag people?

Fan-N-Pick/Showdown

---

13 *The American Colonies*

What religious group formed the Massachusetts Bay Colony?

Fan-N-Pick/Showdown

---

14 *The American Colonies*

What group built the first public school in the English colonies?

Fan-N-Pick/Showdown

---

15 *The American Colonies*

Fan-N-Pick/Showdown

---

16 *The American Colonies*

Fan-N-Pick/Showdown

United States Social Studies: Engaging Cooperative Learning Activities
Kagan Publishing • 800.933.2667 • www.KaganOnline.com

49

The American Colonies
Life in the Colonies

Directions: Copy one set of cards for each team. Cut out each card along the dotted lines. Give each team a set of cards to play Fan-N-Pick or Showdown.

1 *The American Colonies*

What is an apprentice? What might an apprentice job be within a colony?

Fan-N-Pick/Showdown

2 *The American Colonies*

What roles did young girls play in the colonies?

Fan-N-Pick/Showdown

3 *The American Colonies*

What roles did the young boys play in the colonies?

Fan-N-Pick/Showdown

4 *The American Colonies*

If you lived in the New England Colonies, what jobs might you hold?

Fan-N-Pick/Showdown

5 *The American Colonies*

If you lived in the Middle Colonies, what jobs might you hold?

Fan-N-Pick/Showdown

6 *The American Colonies*

If you lived in the Southern Colonies, what jobs might you hold?

Fan-N-Pick/Showdown

7 *The American Colonies*

Which famous inventor helped Philadelphia thrive during the 1700s?

Fan-N-Pick/Showdown

8 *The American Colonies*

What did the Puritans hope to achieve in North America?

Fan-N-Pick/Showdown

United States Social Studies: Engaging Cooperative Learning Activities
Kagan Publishing • 800.933.2667 • www.KaganOnline.com

The American Colonies
Life in the Colonies

Directions: Copy one set of cards for each team. Cut out each card along the dotted lines. Give each team a set of cards to play Fan-N-Pick or Showdown.

---

9 *The American Colonies*

Name two ways that the American Indians and the colonists benefited from each other.

Fan-N-Pick/Showdown

---

10 *The American Colonies*

Name two negative impacts of the colonists moving to the North American continent.

Fan-N-Pick/Showdown

---

11 *The American Colonies*

Which new food introduced by the American Indians proved easy to grow and became a staple food item?

Fan-N-Pick/Showdown

---

12 *The American Colonies*

Name two games that colonists played that are still enjoyed in some version, today.

Fan-N-Pick/Showdown

---

13 *The American Colonies*

Fan-N-Pick/Showdown

---

14 *The American Colonies*

Fan-N-Pick/Showdown

---

15 *The American Colonies*

Fan-N-Pick/Showdown

---

16 *The American Colonies*

Fan-N-Pick/Showdown

United States Social Studies: Engaging Cooperative Learning Activities
Kagan Publishing • 800.933.2667 • www.KaganOnline.com

51

The American Colonies
Guiding New Territories

Directions: Cut out cards along the dotted lines. Distribute one card per student in sequence so for every student with a person, place, or term card, there is a student with a matching description card. Students use cards to play Mix-N-Match.

The American Colonies **John White**	**The American Colonies** Led more than one hundred people to Roanoake Island but returned to England for supplies, and upon his return discovered the colony had disappeared
The American Colonies **Sir Walter Raleigh**	**The American Colonies** Adviser to Queen Elizabeth, agreed to organize the first colony of Roanoake, solider familiar with North America
The American Colonies **Roanoke Island**	**The American Colonies** England's first attempt at creating an American colony, faced difficult times and starvation that caused many to return to England. A second attempt in 1587 proved hard and by August 1590, the colony had mysteriously disappeared.
The American Colonies **Jamestown Colony**	**The American Colonies** Group of merchants formed this colony in 1606, founded in Virginia

United States Social Studies: Engaging Cooperative Learning Activities
Kagan Publishing • 800.933.2667 • www.KaganOnline.com

52

The American Colonies
Guiding New Territories

Directions: Cut out cards along the dotted lines. Distribute one card per student in sequence so for every student with a person, place, or term card, there is a student with a matching description card. Students use cards to play Mix-N-Match.

The American Colonies **Charter** *Mix-N-Match*	**The American Colonies** Document which allowed colonists to settle on new land that was claimed by the ruler of his or her home country *Mix-N-Match*
The American Colonies **John Smith** *Mix-N-Match*	**The American Colonies** Elected leader of Jamestown Colony, traded with leader of the Powhatan Indian people, life saved by Pocahontas *Mix-N-Match*
The American Colonies **Pocahontas** *Mix-N-Match*	**The American Colonies** Young daughter of Chief Powhatan, leader of Powhatan people, at age 12 saved life of John Smith *Mix-N-Match*
The American Colonies **Indentured Servant** *Mix-N-Match*	**The American Colonies** Someone who agrees to work for a set number of years in exchange for the cost of journeying overseas to North America *Mix-N-Match*

United States Social Studies: Engaging Cooperative Learning Activities
Kagan Publishing • 800.933.2667 • www.KaganOnline.com

53

The American Colonies
Guiding New Territories

Directions: Cut out cards along the dotted lines. Distribute one card per student in sequence so for every student with a person, place, or term card, there is a student with a matching description card. Students use cards to play Mix-N-Match.

The American Colonies

House of Burgesses

Mix-N-Match

The American Colonies

First law making assembly in an English colony

Mix-N-Match

The American Colonies

New England Colonies

Mix-N-Match

The American Colonies

Group of colonies known for the first emigrants including Puritan separatists later known as Pilgrims, Massachusetts Bay Company sent large group to establish Massachusetts settlement, also included colonies of Connecticut, Rhode Island, and New Hampshire

Mix-N-Match

The American Colonies

Middle Colonies

Mix-N-Match

The American Colonies

Group of colonies known for being occupied by Dutch traders and landowners, area became known as New York, land West of Delware was given to Quaker William Penn who developed colony eventually known as Pennsylvania

Mix-N-Match

The American Colonies

Southern Colonies

Mix-N-Match

The American Colonies

Group of colonies that began south of Virginia and stretched down to Florida, known for farming and plantations which produced varying crops, relied on African slave labor from Barbados

Mix-N-Match

United States Social Studies: Engaging Cooperative Learning Activities
Kagan Publishing • 800.933.2667 • www.KaganOnline.com

54

The American Revolution

Cooperative Learning Activities

The American Revolution
The Tea Act

Directions: Think about the prompt, and then write your own response. When done, RoundRobin share your writing with your teammates. Use the space at the bottom to record ideas your teammates share.

Prompt: Imagine you are a colonist that has just received news of the Tea Act passed by Parliament. Write a letter to a family member and describe your reaction, thoughts, and feelings to this new law.

My writing: _____

_____

_____

_____

_____

_____

_____

_____

_____

_____

Ideas Teammates Share

United States Social Studies: *Engaging Cooperative Learning Activities*
Kagan Publishing • 800.933.2667 • www.KaganOnline.com

The American Revolution
"Give Me Liberty or Give Me Death!"

Directions: Think about the prompt, and then write your own response. When done, RoundRobin share your writing with your teammates. Use the space at the bottom to record ideas your teammates share.

Prompt: Before declaring war, Patrick Henry gave a speech ending with, *"I know not what course others may take; but as for me, give me liberty or give me death!"* How do these words shape the future for the American government? Explain using details from history.

My writing: _____

_____

_____

_____

_____

_____

_____

_____

_____

_____

Ideas Teammates Share

United States Social Studies: Engaging Cooperative Learning Activities
Kagan Publishing • 800.933.2667 • www.KaganOnline.com

57

The American Revolution
"No Taxation without Representation"

Directions: Think about the prompt, and then write your own response. When done, RoundRobin share your writing with your teammates. Use the space at the bottom to record ideas your teammates share.

Prompt: Describe the phrase "No Taxation without Representation" in regards to the American Revolution. How did this ideal trigger the start of the war?

My writing: _____

_____

_____

_____

_____

_____

_____

_____

_____

_____

_____

_____

Ideas Teammates Share

58

United States Social Studies: Engaging Cooperative Learning Activities
Kagan Publishing • 800.933.2667 • www.KaganOnline.com

The American Revolution
The Battle Begins

■ **RallyCoach Directions:** Take turns answering each question as your partner coaches. Explain your thinking to your coach.

■ **Sage-N-Scribe Directions:** The Sage describes what he or she knows about the question so the Scribe can answer the question. The Sage and Scribe switch roles for each question.

Name _____

1. **What restrictions did the Tea Act place on the colonists?**
   a) Colonists were not allowed to drink British tea.
   b) Tea could only be purchased through the East India Tea Company.
   c) Taxes would not be collected on British tea.
   d) There were higher taxes for all tea purchased or sold regardless of origin.

2. **Colonists who opposed British rule were known as _____.**
   a) Patriots
   b) Loyalists
   c) Soldiers
   d) Minutemen

3. **What caused the British to fire among the minutemen on April 19, 1775?**
   a) An unknown shot was fired.
   b) The colonists refused to return back to their homes.
   c) Paul Revere rode into town yelling, *"The British are coming!"*
   d) King George III ordered any man who belonged to the minutemen executed.

4. **Why were the British soldiers able to successfully win the Battle of Bunker Hill?**
   a) They outnumbered the minutemen by over three times as many soldiers.
   b) The minutemen did not have the proper weapons, and misfiring killed their own men.
   c) The minutemen stayed up all night to prepare the fort and then eventually ran out of ammunition.
   d) The British used advanced weaponry.

Name _____

1. **Which of the following was NOT part of what the colonists called the Intolerable Acts?**
   a) Colony of Massachusetts was placed under the control of Thomas Gage.
   b) British soldiers were sent back to Boston and were to be housed and fed by colonists.
   c) Britain imposed higher taxes and stricter penalties.
   d) The Port of Boston was closed.

2. **Colonists who supported King George III and British rule were known as _____.**
   a) Patriots
   b) Loyalists
   c) Soldiers
   d) Minutemen

3. **What role did women play when the British marched into Concord in 1775?**
   a) The women stood along the battlefield to tend to wounded soldiers.
   b) The women hid all the minutemen's weapons in fields and barns over town so the British wouldn't discover them.
   c) They cooked a special pre-war meal.
   d) They retreated into the woods for safety.

4. **What advice is Colonel Prescott quoted as saying before the Battle of Bunker Hill?**
   a) *"Our fight is for freedom for our sons and daughters!"*
   b) *"Don't fire till you see the whites of their eyes."*
   c) *"This is the start of the war for America."*
   d) *"We fight for life, liberty, and the pursuit of all happiness."*

United States Social Studies: Engaging Cooperative Learning Activities
Kagan Publishing • 800.933.2667 • www.KaganOnline.com

59

The American Revolution
Soldiers and War

■ **RallyCoach Directions:** Take turns answering each question as your partner coaches. Explain your thinking to your coach.
■ **Sage-N-Scribe Directions:** The Sage describes what he or she knows about the question so the Scribe can answer the question. The Sage and Scribe switch roles for each question.

Name _____

1. Why was the war being fought in 1776 between America and Britain?
   a) Britain wanted to gain more citizens.
   b) America was fighting for independence.
   c) Britain wanted to outlaw slavery in all states.
   d) America wanted to be ruled by their own king.

2. Which of the following is not true regarding the American soldiers?
   a) Many had no jackets.
   b) Many men were sick, exhausted, and cold.
   c) Some men marched with rags on their feet.
   d) Everyone was well fed.

3. Where did General George Washington and his men find inspiration to continue fighting?
   a) Letters and care packages from their wives
   b) Songs sang about victory and freedom
   c) The words written by Thomas Paine
   d) Washington's nightly journals

4. The fight against the Hessians became known as _____.
   a) New Jersey Battle
   b) Hessian Slaughter
   c) Battle of Trenton
   d) Fall of the Hessian

5. Washington lined men on the south side of the Assunpink Creek hoping to _____?
   a) Show courage to the British and Hessian
   b) Make a strong stand to win the war now
   c) Slow the enemy down
   d) Gain ammunition and much needed cannons

Name _____

1. Who was the leader of the American Army?
   a) Thomas Paine
   b) Enoch Anderson
   c) James Monroe
   d) George Washington

2. What is a Hessian?
   a) German soldier fighting for the British
   b) American soldier working as a spy for Germany
   c) British soldier removed from fighting
   d) British soldier

3. Why was crossing the Delaware River in winter difficult?
   a) The water was frozen in places and chunks of ice had to be removed.
   b) The water was black and hard to see through.
   c) Men could not easily see to fire across the water.
   d) The water was high and fast moving.

4. Which of the following was the method Washington persuaded his men to return after the new year?
   a) Promised more time home with family
   b) Appealed to the love of the country
   c) Made a speech about the dangers of Britain
   d) Provided new coats and shoes for the men

5. Which of the following words best describes General George Washington?
   a) Courageous
   b) Foolish
   c) Follower
   d) Honest

60

United States Social Studies: Engaging Cooperative Learning Activities
Kagan Publishing • 800.933.2667 • www.KaganOnline.com

The American Revolution
Politics and Government

Directions: Cut out each card along the dotted lines. Then fold each card in half so the question is on one side and the answer is on the back. Glue or tape the cards together to keep the answers and questions on opposite sides.

1 *The American Revolution*

What is the name of the governing body in Great Britain?

a) Commoners System
b) House of Lords
c) King George Court
d) British Parliament

Quiz-Quiz-Trade • Question

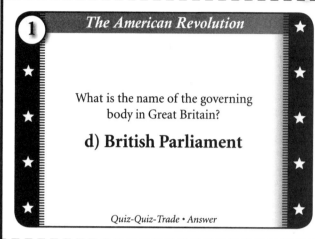

1 *The American Revolution*

What is the name of the governing body in Great Britain?

d) British Parliament

Quiz-Quiz-Trade • Answer

2 *The American Revolution*

Why did Parliament pass a Sugar Act and Stamp Act?

a) To collect taxes to help pay for Great Britain's war debt
b) To prevent colonists from earning too much money
c) To remind colonists that Great Britain would remain the world power
d) To limit the sale and consumption of sugar and prevent men from playing cards

Quiz-Quiz-Trade • Question

2 *The American Revolution*

Why did Parliament pass a Sugar Act and Stamp Act?

a) To collect taxes to help pay for Great Britain's war debt

Quiz-Quiz-Trade • Answer

3 *The American Revolution*

What does the phrase "no taxation without representation" mean?

a) Men would only be taxed when they shopped in person.
b) Taxes could be raised and collected even if no one worked in Parliament.
c) Citizens could never be taxed unless their elected representative voted to pay.
d) The British king had to collect taxes in person.

Quiz-Quiz-Trade • Question

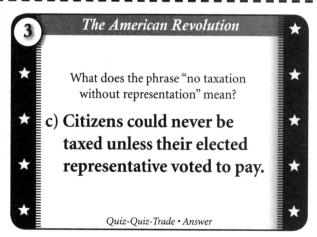

3 *The American Revolution*

What does the phrase "no taxation without representation" mean?

c) Citizens could never be taxed unless their elected representative voted to pay.

Quiz-Quiz-Trade • Answer

United States Social Studies: Engaging Cooperative Learning Activities
Kagan Publishing • 800.933.2667 • www.KaganOnline.com

61

The American Revolution
Politics and Government

Directions: Cut out each card along the dotted lines. Then fold each card in half so the question is on one side and the answer is on the back. Glue or tape the cards together to keep the answers and questions on opposite sides.

4 *The American Revolution*

Which of the following is NOT one way the colonists fought the taxes by Great Britain?

a) Smuggled in untaxed goods from other countries
b) Banned sale of all items taxed by Great Britain
c) Shot tax collectors at the door
d) Made own goods instead of buying British ones

Quiz-Quiz-Trade • Question

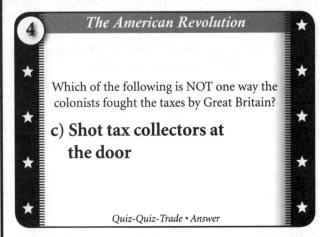

4 *The American Revolution*

Which of the following is NOT one way the colonists fought the taxes by Great Britain?

c) Shot tax collectors at the door

Quiz-Quiz-Trade • Answer

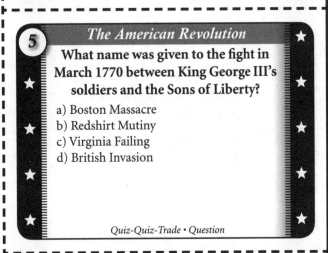

5 *The American Revolution*

What name was given to the fight in March 1770 between King George III's soldiers and the Sons of Liberty?

a) Boston Massacre
b) Redshirt Mutiny
c) Virginia Failing
d) British Invasion

Quiz-Quiz-Trade • Question

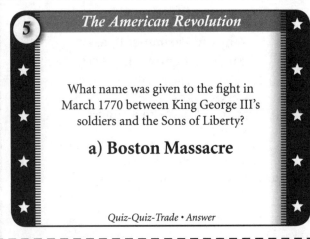

5 *The American Revolution*

What name was given to the fight in March 1770 between King George III's soldiers and the Sons of Liberty?

a) Boston Massacre

Quiz-Quiz-Trade • Answer

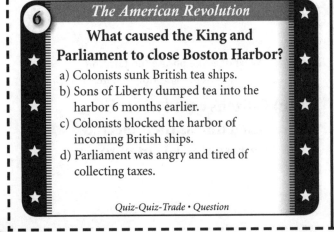

6 *The American Revolution*

What caused the King and Parliament to close Boston Harbor?

a) Colonists sunk British tea ships.
b) Sons of Liberty dumped tea into the harbor 6 months earlier.
c) Colonists blocked the harbor of incoming British ships.
d) Parliament was angry and tired of collecting taxes.

Quiz-Quiz-Trade • Question

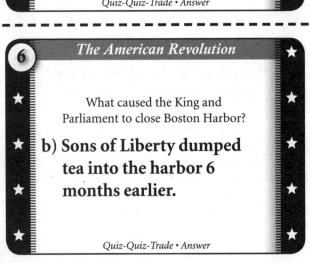

6 *The American Revolution*

What caused the King and Parliament to close Boston Harbor?

b) Sons of Liberty dumped tea into the harbor 6 months earlier.

Quiz-Quiz-Trade • Answer

United States Social Studies: Engaging Cooperative Learning Activities
Kagan Publishing • 800.933.2667 • www.KaganOnline.com

62

The American Revolution
Politics and Government

Directions: Cut out each card along the dotted lines. Then fold each card in half so the question is on one side and the answer is on the back. Glue or tape the cards together to keep the answers and questions on opposite sides.

7 *The American Revolution*

What was an effect of the Boston Harbor being shut down?

a) Great Britain realized they could not win a war.
b) Tea taxes continued to soar.
c) A huge number of Bostonians were out of work.
d) George Washington was made Harbor Captain.

Quiz-Quiz-Trade • Question

7 *The American Revolution*

What was an effect of the Boston Harbor being shut down?

c) A huge number of Bostonians were out of work.

Quiz-Quiz-Trade • Answer

8 *The American Revolution*

Until Parliament agreed to get rid of all unconstitutional laws controlling America, the colonies _____.

a) would continue to get tea and goods from Holland
b) would only pay taxes on paper goods
c) would not attend any meetings with Great Britain
d) would not import British goods or export their goods to the mother country

Quiz-Quiz-Trade • Question

8 *The American Revolution*

Until Parliament agreed to get rid of all unconstitutional laws controlling America, the colonies _____.

d) Would not import British goods or export their goods to the mother country

Quiz-Quiz-Trade • Answer

9 *The American Revolution*

What name is given to the first shot fired in Concord that is said to have been the start of the Revolutionary War?

a) British Protest
b) Revolutionary Rifle
c) The Shot Heard Round the World
d) Shots on America

Quiz-Quiz-Trade • Question

9 *The American Revolution*

What name is given to the first shot fired in Concord that is said to have been the start of the Revolutionary War?

c) The Shot Heard Round the World

Quiz-Quiz-Trade • Answer

United States Social Studies: Engaging Cooperative Learning Activities
Kagan Publishing • 800.933.2667 • www.KaganOnline.com

63

The American Revolution
Politics and Government

Directions: Cut out each card along the dotted lines. Then fold each card in half so the question is on one side and the answer is on the back. Glue or tape the cards together to keep the answers and questions on opposite sides.

---

10 *The American Revolution* ★

What was a result of the meeting of the Second Continental Congress?

a) George Washington was chosen to become Commander-in-Chief of the newly chosen Continental Army.
b) The U.S. Constitution was written and sent to King George III as a list of demands.
c) The men at the meeting decided Great Britain needed to refund all of the taxes collected.
d) Americans decided the war could not be won and would rather make peace with Great Britain.

Quiz-Quiz-Trade • Question

---

10 *The American Revolution* ★

What was a result of the meeting of the Second Continental Congress?

a) George Washington was chosen to become Commander-in-Chief of the newly chosen Continental Army.

Quiz-Quiz-Trade • Answer

---

11 *The American Revolution* ★

What is the name of the document that was written in 1776 that declared America free from British rule and listed the grievances towards King George III?

a) U.S. Constitution
b) Bill of Rights
c) Declaration of Independence
d) War and Peace

Quiz-Quiz-Trade • Question

---

11 *The American Revolution* ★

What is the name of the document that was written in 1776 that declared America free from British rule and listed the grievances towards King George III?

c) Declaration of Independence

Quiz-Quiz-Trade • Answer

---

12 *The American Revolution* ★

Who are the Hessians?

a) Highly trained German troops paid to fight for the British
b) Senior officers and noblemen from Great Britain
c) Naval officers and the guard to the prince of England
d) Soldiers who did not follow the rules of war and fought with the colonists against the British

Quiz-Quiz-Trade • Question

---

12 *The American Revolution* ★

Who are the Hessians?

a) Highly trained German troops paid to fight for the British.

Quiz-Quiz-Trade • Answer

United States Social Studies: Engaging Cooperative Learning Activities
Kagan Publishing • 800.933.2667 • www.KaganOnline.com

64

The American Revolution
Politics and Government

Directions: Cut out each card along the dotted lines. Then fold each card in half so the question is on one side and the answer is on the back. Glue or tape the cards together to keep the answers and questions on opposite sides.

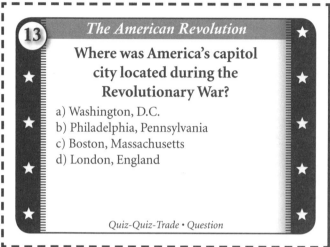

13 The American Revolution

Where was America's capitol city located during the Revolutionary War?

a) Washington, D.C.
b) Philadelphia, Pennsylvania
c) Boston, Massachusetts
d) London, England

Quiz-Quiz-Trade • Question

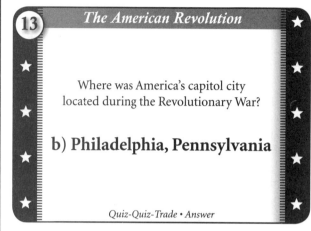

13 The American Revolution

Where was America's capitol city located during the Revolutionary War?

b) Philadelphia, Pennsylvania

Quiz-Quiz-Trade • Answer

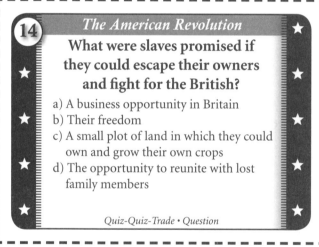

14 The American Revolution

What were slaves promised if they could escape their owners and fight for the British?

a) A business opportunity in Britain
b) Their freedom
c) A small plot of land in which they could own and grow their own crops
d) The opportunity to reunite with lost family members

Quiz-Quiz-Trade • Question

14 The American Revolution

What were slaves promised if they could escape their owners and fight for the British?

b) Their freedom

Quiz-Quiz-Trade • Answer

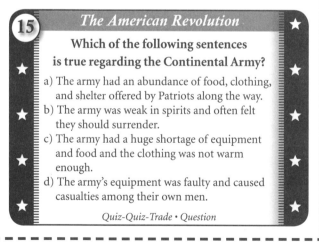

15 The American Revolution

Which of the following sentences is true regarding the Continental Army?

a) The army had an abundance of food, clothing, and shelter offered by Patriots along the way.
b) The army was weak in spirits and often felt they should surrender.
c) The army had a huge shortage of equipment and food and the clothing was not warm enough.
d) The army's equipment was faulty and caused casualties among their own men.

Quiz-Quiz-Trade • Question

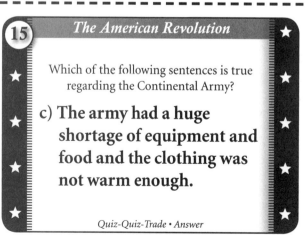

15 The American Revolution

Which of the following sentences is true regarding the Continental Army?

c) The army had a huge shortage of equipment and food and the clothing was not warm enough.

Quiz-Quiz-Trade • Answer

United States Social Studies: Engaging Cooperative Learning Activities
Kagan Publishing • 800.933.2667 • www.KaganOnline.com

65

The American Revolution
Politics and Government

Directions: Cut out each card along the dotted lines. Then fold each card in half so the question is on one side and the answer is on the back. Glue or tape the cards together to keep the answers and questions on opposite sides.

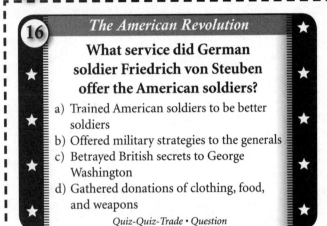

16

The American Revolution

What service did German soldier Friedrich von Steuben offer the American soldiers?

a) Trained American soldiers to be better soldiers
b) Offered military strategies to the generals
c) Betrayed British secrets to George Washington
d) Gathered donations of clothing, food, and weapons

Quiz-Quiz-Trade • Question

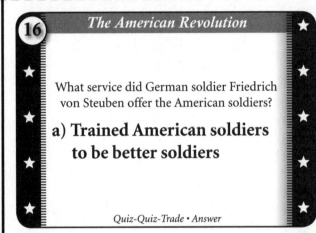

16

The American Revolution

What service did German soldier Friedrich von Steuben offer the American soldiers?

a) Trained American soldiers to be better soldiers

Quiz-Quiz-Trade • Answer

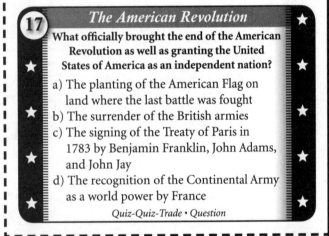

17

The American Revolution

What officially brought the end of the American Revolution as well as granting the United States of America as an independent nation?

a) The planting of the American Flag on land where the last battle was fought
b) The surrender of the British armies
c) The signing of the Treaty of Paris in 1783 by Benjamin Franklin, John Adams, and John Jay
d) The recognition of the Continental Army as a world power by France

Quiz-Quiz-Trade • Question

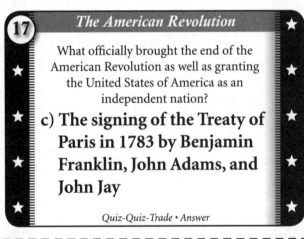

17

The American Revolution

What officially brought the end of the American Revolution as well as granting the United States of America as an independent nation?

c) The signing of the Treaty of Paris in 1783 by Benjamin Franklin, John Adams, and John Jay

Quiz-Quiz-Trade • Answer

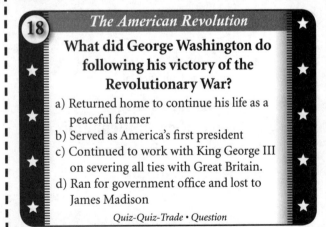

18

The American Revolution

What did George Washington do following his victory of the Revolutionary War?

a) Returned home to continue his life as a peaceful farmer
b) Served as America's first president
c) Continued to work with King George III on severing all ties with Great Britain.
d) Ran for government office and lost to James Madison

Quiz-Quiz-Trade • Question

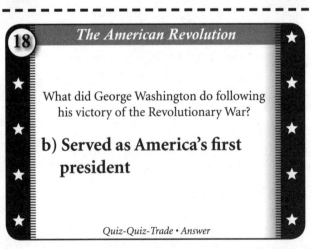

18

The American Revolution

What did George Washington do following his victory of the Revolutionary War?

b) Served as America's first president

Quiz-Quiz-Trade • Answer

The American Revolution
Congressional Acts

Name: _____

Directions: Pair up and take turns circling the answer to each question. Don't forget to get your partner's initials.

 1

Which of the following was a reason for Britain's higher taxes such as the Stamp Act?

a) Britain was afraid of the colonists' demands for independence.
b) The French and Indian War was very costly.
c) Britain was suffering from food shortages.
d) The colonies were expanding so rapidly.

_____
Initials

 2

What was the Stamp Act of 1765?

a) A tax on printed materials in the colonies
b) A tax of any material with a British stamp
c) A tax on imported goods from countries other than Britain
d) A tax the government charged for legal documents

_____
Initials

 3

Who is cited as one of the first people to publicly speak out against the Stamp Act?

a) James Monroe
b) Abraham Lincoln
c) Martha Washington
d) Patrick Henry

_____
Initials

 4

What was a result of repealing the Stamp Act?

a) The Townshend Acts took its place.
b) Stamp Tax collectors were hung in the town square.
c) Britain declared war on the colonists.
d) Patrick Henry was jailed for treason.

_____
Initials

 5

Which of the following was NOT an effect following Britain's implementation of taxes?

a) Colonial women made "liberty tea" rather than pay taxes on British tea.
b) Colonists boycotted British goods.
c) Colonists threatened tax collectors.
d) Britain raised taxes in their homeland.

_____
Initials

 6

Which group was founded by Samuel Adams in protest against British taxes?

a) Continental Congress
b) Stamp Act Congress
c) Colonist Heroes
d) Sons of Liberty

_____
Initials

 7

What was the result of heightened tension in Boston causing soldiers to panic?

a) The Boston Tea Party
b) The Boston Massacre
c) Intolerable Acts
d) Daughters of Liberty

_____
Initials

8

What did the Townshend Acts establish?

a) A sentence of treason for not paying a tax
b) A tariff or tax on imported goods
c) Lower taxes for colonists pledging loyalty to Britain
d) A boycott on goods from colonists

_____
Initials

9

What was the solution to slow news travel among colonies?

a) Committee of Correspondence
b) Development of the telegraph
c) Midnight Riders
d) Secret colonist newspapers

_____
Initials

United States Social Studies: Engaging Cooperative Learning Activities
Kagan Publishing • 800.933.2667 • www.KaganOnline.com

67

The American Revolution
Separation from Britain

Name: _____

Directions: Pair up and take turns answering each question. Don't forget to get your partner's initials.

1 Who was chosen to lead the newly formed American army?

_____
_____
_____
_____

_____
Initials

2 What name was given to the newly formed American army?

_____
_____
_____
_____

_____
Initials

3 Who served as the president of the Second Continental Congress?

_____
_____
_____
_____

_____
Initials

4 What name was given to the first document, still pledging loyalty to Britain in exchange for greater freedom to govern themselves, sent to King George III in July 1775?

_____
_____

_____
Initials

5 Who was the author of the pamphlet known as *Common Sense*, arguing for separation for Britain?

_____
_____
_____

_____
Initials

6 Who was the main author of the Declaration of Independence?

_____
_____
_____

_____
Initials

7 On what date was the Declaration of Independence formally approved?

_____
_____
_____
_____

_____
Initials

8 What name was given to the German missionaries hired by King George III?

_____
_____
_____

_____
Initials

9 What battle, often thought of as a turning point in the war for the Americans, ended with British soldiers surrendering on October 17, 1776?

_____
_____

_____
Initials

United States Social Studies: Engaging Cooperative Learning Activities
Kagan Publishing • 800.933.2667 • www.KaganOnline.com

The American Revolution
Dates and Events

Name: _____

Events
• Boston Tea Party   • Washington takes command of Continental Army

Events

- Boston Tea Party
- Stamp Act goes into effect
- Second Continental Congress
- Shot Heard Round the World
- King Louis XVI of France signed treaty
- Washington takes command of Continental Army
- Washington and troops won Second Battle of Trenton
- England signed peace treaty declaring total independence
- George Washington chosen president of Constitutional Convention

Directions: Pair up and take turns using the events in the box above to answer each question. Don't forget to get your partner's initials.

1
What event happened on December 16, 1773?
_____
_____
_____
_____ Initials

2
What event happened on April 19, 1775?
_____
_____
_____
_____ Initials

3
What event happened on June 15, 1776?
_____
_____
_____
_____ Initials

4
What event happened on July 3, 1775?
_____
_____
_____
_____ Initials

5
What event happened on January 2, 1777?
_____
_____
_____
_____ Initials

6
What event happened on February 6, 1778?
_____
_____
_____
_____ Initials

7
What event happened on September 3, 1783?
_____
_____
_____
_____ Initials

8
What event happened in May 1787?
_____
_____
_____
_____ Initials

9
What event happened in November 1765?
_____
_____
_____
_____ Initials

The American Revolution
Cause and Effect

Directions: Cut out cards along the dotted lines. Distribute one card per student in sequence so for every student with a Cause card, there is a student with a matching Effect card. Students use cards to play Mix-N-Match.

The American Revolution Cause: **French and Indian War**	*The American Revolution* Effect: **Parliament passed the Stamp Act**
The American Revolution Cause: **The Stamp Act**	*The American Revolution* Effect: **Sons of Liberty formed**
The American Revolution Cause: **Parliament repealed the Stamp Act**	*The American Revolution* Effect: **Parliament passed the Townshend Acts**
The American Revolution Cause: **The Townshend Acts**	*The American Revolution* Effect: **Colonist boycotted British goods**

Mix-N-Match (card side labels)

70

United States Social Studies: *Engaging Cooperative Learning Activities*
Kagan Publishing • 800.933.2667 • www.KaganOnline.com

The American Revolution
Cause and Effect

Directions: Cut out cards along the dotted lines. Distribute one card per student in sequence so for every student with a Cause card, there is a student with a matching Effect card. Students use cards to play Mix-N-Match.

The American Revolution Cause: **Rising tension in Boston in 1776** *Mix-N-Match*	*The American Revolution* Effect: **Boston Massacre** *Mix-N-Match*
The American Revolution Cause: **Colonial boycotts hurt British businesses** *Mix-N-Match*	*The American Revolution* Effect: **Britain cancels all taxes except the tea tax** *Mix-N-Match*
The American Revolution Cause: **Parliament passes the Tea Act** *Mix-N-Match*	*The American Revolution* Effect: **Boston Tea Party** *Mix-N-Match*
The American Revolution Cause: **Boston Tea Party** *Mix-N-Match*	*The American Revolution* Effect: **The Intolerable Acts** *Mix-N-Match*

United States Social Studies: Engaging Cooperative Learning Activities
Kagan Publishing • 800.933.2667 • www.KaganOnline.com

71

The American Revolution
Cause and Effect

Directions: Cut out cards along the dotted lines. Distribute one card per student in sequence so for every student with a Cause card, there is a student with a matching Effect card. Students use cards to play Mix-N-Match.

The American Revolution

Cause:

The Intolerable Acts

Mix-N-Match

The American Revolution

Effect:

Colonists took sides as Patriots or Loyalists

Mix-N-Match

The American Revolution

Cause:

First Continental Congress

Mix-N-Match

The American Revolution

Effect:

Colonist began training militia

Mix-N-Match

The American Revolution

Cause:

On April 19, 1775, an unknown shot was fired in Lexington, Virginia.

Mix-N-Match

The American Revolution

Effect:
British soldiers opened fire on the minutemen and war broke out. This became known as "the shot heard round the world."

Mix-N-Match

The American Revolution

Cause:

King George III refused to read the Olive Branch Petition

Mix-N-Match

The American Revolution

Effect:

The Second Continental Congress wrote the Declaration of Independence

Mix-N-Match

72

United States Social Studies: Engaging Cooperative Learning Activities
Kagan Publishing • 800.933.2667 • www.KaganOnline.com

The American Revolution
Key People, Terms, and Events

Directions: Copy cards, one per student. Cut out each card along the dotted lines and follow the directions for Who Am I?

① The American Revolution

Stamp Act

Who Am I?

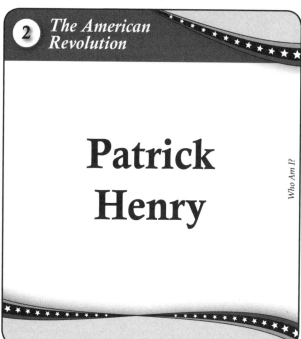

② The American Revolution

Patrick Henry

Who Am I?

③ The American Revolution

Boston Tea Party

Who Am I?

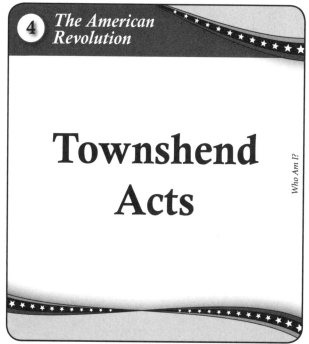

④ The American Revolution

Townshend Acts

Who Am I?

United States Social Studies: Engaging Cooperative Learning Activities
Kagan Publishing • 800.933.2667 • www.KaganOnline.com

73

The American Revolution
Key People, Terms, and Events

Directions: Copy cards, one per student. Cut out each card along the dotted lines and follow the directions for Who Am I?

5 *The American Revolution*

Samuel Adams

Who Am I?

6 *The American Revolution*

Boston Massacre

Who Am I?

7 *The American Revolution*

East India Tea Company

Who Am I?

8 *The American Revolution*

Sons of Liberty

Who Am I?

United States Social Studies: Engaging Cooperative Learning Activities
Kagan Publishing • 800.933.2667 • www.KaganOnline.com

The American Revolution
Key People, Terms, and Events

Directions: Copy cards, one per student. Cut out each card along the dotted lines and follow the directions for Who Am I?

9 *The American Revolution*

Liberty Tea

Who Am I?

10 *The American Revolution*

Stamp Act Congress

Who Am I?

11 *The American Revolution*

First Continental Congress

Who Am I?

12 *The American Revolution*

Committee of Correspondence

Who Am I?

United States Social Studies: Engaging Cooperative Learning Activities
Kagan Publishing • 800.933.2667 • www.KaganOnline.com

75

The American Revolution
Key People, Terms, and Events

Directions: Copy cards, one per student. Cut out each card along the dotted lines and follow the directions for Who Am I?

13 *The American Revolution*

Paul Revere

Who Am I?

14 *The American Revolution*

Daughters of Liberty

Who Am I?

15 *The American Revolution*

Tea Act

Who Am I?

16 *The American Revolution*

Patriots

Who Am I?

The American Revolution
Key People, Terms, and Events

Directions: Copy cards, one per student. Cut out each card along the dotted lines and follow the directions for Who Am I?

17 *The American Revolution*

Loyalists

Who Am I?

18 *The American Revolution*

Minutemen

Who Am I?

19 *The American Revolution*

Battle of Bunker Hill

Who Am I?

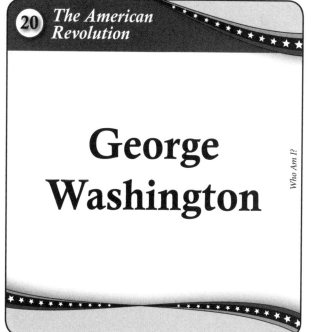

20 *The American Revolution*

George Washington

Who Am I?

United States Social Studies: Engaging Cooperative Learning Activities
Kagan Publishing • 800.933.2667 • www.KaganOnline.com

77

The American Revolution
Key People, Terms, and Events

Directions: Copy cards, one per student. Cut out each card along the dotted lines and follow the directions for Who Am I?

21 *The American Revolution*

Continental Army

Who Am I?

22 *The American Revolution*

John Adams

Who Am I?

23 *The American Revolution*

John Hancock

Who Am I?

24 *The American Revolution*

Thomas Paine

Who Am I?

United States Social Studies: Engaging Cooperative Learning Activities
Kagan Publishing • 800.933.2667 • www.KaganOnline.com

The American Revolution
Key People, Terms, and Events

Directions: Copy cards, one per student. Cut out each card along the dotted lines and follow the directions for Who Am I?

---

25 *The American Revolution*

Declaration of Independence

Who Am I?

---

26 *The American Revolution*

Thomas Jefferson

Who Am I?

---

27 *The American Revolution*

Hessian

Who Am I?

---

28 *The American Revolution*

Battle of Saratoga

Who Am I?

United States Social Studies: Engaging Cooperative Learning Activities
Kagan Publishing • 800.933.2667 • www.KaganOnline.com

79

The American Revolution
Key People, Terms, and Events

Directions: Copy cards, one per student. Cut out each card along the dotted lines and follow the directions for Who Am I?

29 *The American Revolution*

Benedict Arnold

Who Am I?

30 *The American Revolution*

Friedrich von Steuben

Who Am I?

31 *The American Revolution*

Treaty of Paris

Who Am I?

32 *The American Revolution*

Benjamin Franklin

Who Am I?

80

United States Social Studies: Engaging Cooperative Learning Activities
Kagan Publishing • 800.933.2667 • www.KaganOnline.com

The American Revolution
Fighting the War

Directions: The class "mixes" until the teacher calls, "pair." Students find a new partner to discuss or answer the teacher's question.

---

1 *The American Revolution*

How were King George III and George Washington alike?

Mix-Pair-Share

---

2 *The American Revolution*

How were King George III and George Washington different?

Mix-Pair-Share

---

3 *The American Revolution*

How was Great Britain's fighting style different from the American colonists?

Mix-Pair-Share

---

4 *The American Revolution*

How was Great Britain's fighting style similar to the American colonists?

Mix-Pair-Share

---

5 *The American Revolution*

Would you rather fight under George Washington's army or King George III's army? Explain why.

Mix-Pair-Share

---

6 *The American Revolution*

How would the Revolutionary War have been different if the American colonists had more soldiers at the beginning?

Mix-Pair-Share

---

7 *The American Revolution*

How would the Revolutionary War have been different had there not been an ocean separating the American colonists and British?

Mix-Pair-Share

---

8 *The American Revolution*

In your opinion, what was the hardest part about an American soldier's life?

Mix-Pair-Share

United States Social Studies: Engaging Cooperative Learning Activities
Kagan Publishing • 800.933.2667 • www.KaganOnline.com

81

The American Revolution
Fighting the War

Directions: The class "mixes" until the teacher calls, "pair." Students find a new partner to discuss or answer the teacher's question.

---

9 *The American Revolution*

In your opinion, what was the hardest part about a British soldier's life?

Mix-Pair-Share

---

10 *The American Revolution*

How did the Revolutionary War affect families living near the fighting?

Mix-Pair-Share

---

11 *The American Revolution*

If you were an American colonist, would you volunteer to fight under George Washington? Explain your reasoning.

Mix-Pair-Share

---

12 *The American Revolution*

In your opinion, who was the better leader of his army: George Washington or King George III? Explain your thinking.

Mix-Pair-Share

---

13 *The American Revolution*

Mix-Pair-Share

---

14 *The American Revolution*

Mix-Pair-Share

---

15 *The American Revolution*

Mix-Pair-Share

---

16 *The American Revolution*

Mix-Pair-Share

82

United States Social Studies: Engaging Cooperative Learning Activities
Kagan Publishing • 800.933.2667 • www.KaganOnline.com

Historic Documents

Cooperative Learning Activities

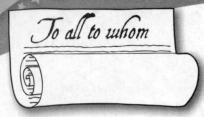
To all to whom

Historic Documents
The Articles of Confederation

■ **RallyCoach Directions:** Take turns answering each question as your partner coaches. Explain your thinking to your coach.
■ **Sage-N-Scribe Directions:** The Sage describes what he or she knows about the question so the Scribe can answer the question. The Sage and Scribe switch roles for each question.

Name _____

1. **What was the purpose of the Articles of Confederation?**
   a) To declare independence from government rule
   b) To outline the plan for the new national government
   c) To state the rights granted to the American people
   d) To seek justice for crimes committed against America

2. **What did the Articles of Confederation do?**
   a) Developed national court system
   b) created a checks and balances system
   c) provided separate power to the states
   d) created a central government

3. **What event proved the need for a stronger national government than outlined in the Articles of Confederation?**
   a) Million man march from Philadelphia, Pennsylvania, to Washington, D.C.
   b) Threat of succession from certain states
   c) Shay's Rebellion and raids in Massachusetts
   d) Lack of funding from unpaid taxes

4. **What was unique about the government while the Confederation was in rule?**
   a) The states held less power than the central government
   b) Each law or rule must be passed by majority of American people
   c) There was no president or monarch in power
   d) The laws were not written down but rather passed through word of mouth

Name _____

1. **What needed to happen in order to put the Articles of Confederation plan into action?**
   a) All thirteen states had to ratify, or approve, it
   b) The British government needed to respond in writing
   c) It had to be signed by George Washington
   d) Approved by the countries that assisted in the defeat of Britain

2. **In order for a major law to be passed, how many state votes were needed?**
   a) All thirteen states
   b) State majority with seven states
   c) Nine states
   d) Ten states

3. **Under the Articles of Confederation, which of the following was NOT something the government could do?**
   a) Coin and borrow money
   b) Create and collect taxes
   c) Declare war and make peace
   d) Operate post offices

4. **How long did the Articles of Confederation last?**
   a) 9 years
   b) 8 years
   c) 7 years
   d) 6 years

Historic Documents
The U.S. Constitution

■ **RallyCoach Directions:** Take turns answering each question as your partner coaches. Explain your thinking to your coach.
■ **Sage-N-Scribe Directions:** The Sage describes what he or she knows about the question so the Scribe can answer the question. The Sage and Scribe switch roles for each question.

Name _____

1. When did the United States become a new country?
   a) 1783
   b) Before the Revolutionary War
   c) 1973
   d) Immediately following the War of 1812

2. What was the Constitutional Convention?
   a) The newspaper that delivered the news
   b) The name of a building
   c) A group of protesters
   d) A special meeting in Philadelphia

3. Who presented the "Virginia Plan"?
   a) George Washington
   b) James Madison
   c) Thomas Jefferson
   d) James Henry

4. What is NOT a reason the meeting rooms were so hot?
   a) The air conditioner was broken.
   b) It was summer.
   c) The windows were shut to keep privacy.
   d) The men wore coats, hats, and wigs.

5. What is the purpose of the seven articles?
   a) To share the state's power
   b) To provide definitions to confusing words
   c) To explain how the government works
   d) To outline a plan of action

Name _____

1. How many states were there when the U.S. Constitution was written?
   a) Fifty
   b) Thirteen
   c) Thirty
   d) Fifteen

2. What name was given to the group of men who helped write the U.S. Constitution?
   a) Founding Fathers
   b) Famous Americans
   c) Constitutional Authors
   d) Change Team

3. Why were the small states unhappy with the new plan?
   a) Small states held too much power.
   b) The government would lose control.
   c) Small states should have as many votes as large states.
   d) Large states had too many people.

4. What are the first words of the U.S. Constitution?
   a) "By the power of the United States,"
   b) "We the People,"
   c) "On this hot summer day,"
   d) "America, the beautiful"

5. When was the U.S. Constitution finally finished?
   a) July 4, 1776
   b) September 17, 1787
   c) October 12, 1592
   d) December 25, 1778

United States Social Studies: Engaging Cooperative Learning Activities
Kagan Publishing • 800.933.2667 • www.KaganOnline.com

85

Historic Documents
The U.S. Constitution

Directions: Copy one set of cards for each team. Cut out each card along the dotted lines. Give each team a set of cards to play Fan-N-Pick or Showdown.

1 Historic Documents

What war did the United States win in order to need its own set of rules?

Fan-N-Pick/Showdown

2 Historic Documents

What was the Constitutional Convention?

Fan-N-Pick/Showdown

3 Historic Documents

What did the Founding Fathers do to help keep the meetings private?

Fan-N-Pick/Showdown

4 Historic Documents

Who was in charge of the Founding Fathers?

Fan-N-Pick/Showdown

5 Historic Documents

What did some people fear could be a problem if the government was too big?

Fan-N-Pick/Showdown

6 Historic Documents

Which part of Congress allowed states an equal number of members?

Fan-N-Pick/Showdown

7 Historic Documents

What is the purpose of the Bill of Rights?

Fan-N-Pick/Showdown

8 Historic Documents

When did the last state agree to the U.S. Constitution?

Fan-N-Pick/Showdown

9 Historic Documents

When was the Bill of Rights added to the U.S. Constitution?

Fan-N-Pick/Showdown

10 Historic Documents

Which state was the first to agree to the U.S. Constitution?

Fan-N-Pick/Showdown

United States Social Studies: Engaging Cooperative Learning Activities
Kagan Publishing • 800.933.2667 • www.KaganOnline.com

Historic Documents
The Declaration of Independence

Name: _____

Directions: Pair up and take turns circling the answer to each question. Don't forget to get your partner's initials.

1 Who was the main author of the Declaration of Independence?

a) George Washington
b) Patrick Henry
c) Thomas Jefferson
d) James Monroe

Initials

2 Whom of the following was NOT on the committee to draft the declaration?

a) James Monroe
b) John Adams
c) Ben Franklin
d) Roger Sherman

Initials

3 What date did the Continental Congress adopt the Declaration of Independence?

a) December 25, 1775
b) July 4, 1776
c) September 17, 1776
d) June 14, 1776

Initials

4 Whose signature is almost five inches long and was the first to sign the Declaration of Independence?

a) John Hancock
b) Thomas Jefferson
c) Benjamin Franklin
d) Robert Livingston

Initials

5 What name was given to the group chosen to write the Declaration of Independence?

a) Continental Congress
b) Declared Writers
c) Founding Fathers
d) Committee of Five

Initials

6 How many members of Congress signed the Declaration of Independence?

a) 55
b) 65
c) 56
d) 59

Initials

7 Which two signers of the Declaration of Independence became U.S. presidents?

a) John Hancock and Thomas Jefferson
b) Thomas Jefferson and John Adams
c) Robert Livingston and George Washington
d) Roger Sherman and John Adams

Initials

8 Why did Congressman John Dickinson refuse to sign the Declaration?

a) He did not know how to read and therefore would not sign a document.
b) He did not agree with slavery.
c) He hoped for a reconciliation with Britain.
d) He was working for the King and against the Continental Congress.

Initials

9 Where can the Declaration of Independence be found today?

a) Smithsonian Museum
b) Oval Office in the White House
c) Library of Congress
d) National Archives Building in Washington, D.C.

Initials

United States Social Studies: Engaging Cooperative Learning Activities
Kagan Publishing • 800.933.2667 • www.KaganOnline.com

87

Historic Documents
The Bill of Rights

Directions: Cut out cards along the dotted lines. Distribute one card per student in sequence so for every student with an amendment number card, there is a student with a matching description card. Students use cards to play Mix-N-Match.

Historic Documents

What does this amendment state?

First

Mix-N-Match

Historic Documents

Which amendment protects the following?
Freedom of speech, religion, press, assemble peacefully, voice complaints against the government

Mix-N-Match

Historic Documents

What does this amendment state?

Second

Mix-N-Match

Historic Documents

Which amendment protects the following?
Own and bare firearms

Mix-N-Match

Historic Documents

What does this amendment state?

Third

Mix-N-Match

Historic Documents

Which amendment protects the following?
Government cannot force citizens to house soldiers during peacetime.

Mix-N-Match

Historic Documents

What does this amendment state?

Fourth

Mix-N-Match

Historic Documents

Which amendment protects the following?
Unfair search and seizure of property

Mix-N-Match

88

United States Social Studies: Engaging Cooperative Learning Activities
Kagan Publishing • 800.933.2667 • www.KaganOnline.com

Historic Documents
The Bill of Rights

Bill of Rights

Directions: Cut out cards along the dotted lines. Distribute one card per student in sequence so for every student with an amendment number card, there is a student with a matching description card. Students use cards to play Mix-N-Match.

Historical Documents

What does this amendment state?

Fifth

Mix-N-Match

Historic Documents

Which amendment protects the following?
No one can be deprived of life, liberty, and the pursuit of happiness without the decision of the court of law.

Mix-N-Match

Historic Documents

What does this amendment state?

Sixth

Mix-N-Match

Historic Documents

Which amendment protects the following?
Right to trial by jury and a lawyer in criminal cases

Mix-N-Match

Historic Documents

What does this amendment state?

Seventh

Mix-N-Match

Historic Documents

Which amendment protects the following?
Right to trial by jury in most civil cases

Mix-N-Match

Historic Documents

What does this amendment state?

Eighth

Mix-N-Match

Historic Documents

Which amendment protects the following?
Prohibits high bail bonds, extreme punishments, and very high fines

Mix-N-Match

United States Social Studies: Engaging Cooperative Learning Activities
Kagan Publishing • 800.933.2667 • www.KaganOnline.com

89

Historic Documents
The Bill of Rights

Directions: Cut out cards along the dotted lines. Distribute one card per student in sequence so for every student with an amendment number card, there is a student with a matching description card. Students use cards to play Mix-N-Match.

Historic Documents

What does this amendment state?

Nineth

Mix-N-Match

Historic Documents

Which amendment protects the following?
Rights of people are not limited to those stated in the Constitution.

Mix-N-Match

Historic Documents

What does this amendment state?

Tenth

Mix-N-Match

Historic Documents

Which amendment protects the following?
Powers not granted to the federal government are decided by the state government or the people.

Mix-N-Match

United States Social Studies: Engaging Cooperative Learning Activities
Kagan Publishing • 800.933.2667 • www.KaganOnline.com

Historic Documents
The Declaration of Independence

Directions: The class "mixes" until the teacher calls, "pair." Students find a new partner to discuss or answer the teacher's question.

---

① *Historic Documents*

What do these words from
the **Declaration of Independence** mean to you?

"We hold these truths to be self-evident, that all men are created equal,"

Mix-Pair-Share

---

② *Historic Documents*

In your opinion what is the most important word found in the Declaration of Independence? Explain your thinking.

Mix-Pair-Share

---

③ *Historic Documents*

What was the overall impact of the Declaration of Independence on our nation? Explain.

Mix-Pair-Share

---

④ *Historic Documents*

What do these words from
the **Declaration of Independence** mean to you?

"…that they (all men), are endowed by their Creator with certain unalienable Rights, that among these are Life, Liberty and the pursuit of Happiness."

Mix-Pair-Share

---

⑤ *Historic Documents*

Read these words from the **Declaration of Independence**. What unalienable right is most important to you? Explain.

"…that they (all men), are endowed by their Creator with certain unalienable Rights, that among these are Life, Liberty and the pursuit of Happiness."

Mix-Pair-Share

---

⑥ *Historic Documents*

Read these words from the **Declaration of Independence**. What government action(s) might cause the people to alter or abolish a current form of government?

"That whatever any Form of Government becomes destructive of these ends, it is the Right of the People to alter or to abolish it, and to institute new Government,"

Mix-Pair-Share

---

⑦ *Historic Documents*

Imagine yourself as a Founding Father of the United States of America. What would be your reason for writing the **Declaration of Independence**?

Mix-Pair-Share

---

⑧ *Historic Documents*

What do these words from the **Declaration of Independence** mean when related to school?

"We hold these truths to be self-evident, that all men are created equal,"

Mix-Pair-Share

United States Social Studies: Engaging Cooperative Learning Activities
Kagan Publishing • 800.933.2667 • www.KaganOnline.com

91

Historic Documents
The Declaration of Independence

Directions: The class "mixes" until the teacher calls, "pair." Students find a new partner to discuss or answer the teacher's question.

---

9 *Historic Documents*

What do these words from the **Declaration of Independence** mean to you?

"That to secure these rights, Governments are instituted among Men, deriving their just powers from the consent of the governed,"

Mix-Pair-Share

---

10 *Historic Documents*

The Declaration of Independence was written in 1776. If you could change, add, or delete anything about it to fit today's world, what changes would you make? Explain your thinking.

Mix-Pair-Share

---

11 *Historic Documents*

Why is the Declaration of Independence an important historic document in our nation? In your opinion, what does this mean to you? Explain.

Mix-Pair-Share

---

12 *Historic Documents*

Imagine you were a colonist during the writing of the Declaration of Independence. What feelings, for or against, might you be feeling towards the writing of this document? Share your thinking.

Mix-Pair-Share

---

13 *Historic Documents*

The Declaration of Independence begins with "The unanimous Declaration of the thirteen united States of America…" What reason might Thomas Jefferson had for beginning this way? Was it necessary or unnecessary? Explain.

Mix-Pair-Share

---

14 *Historic Documents*

Part of the Declaration of Independence lists grievances against the King as reasons for writing the document.

What grievance do you think was the most important? Explain.

Mix-Pair-Share

---

15 *Historic Documents*

Mix-Pair-Share

---

16 *Historic Documents*

Mix-Pair-Share

92

United States Social Studies: Engaging Cooperative Learning Activities
Kagan Publishing • 800.933.2667 • www.KaganOnline.com

Formation of a New Government

Cooperative Learning Activities

Formation of a New Government
Judicial Branch

Directions: Think about the prompt, and then write your own response. When done, RoundRobin share your writing with your teammates. Use the space at the bottom to record ideas your teammates share.

Prompt

The judicial branch interprets the Constitution through the court system. How does the court system protect the rights of American citizens?

My Writing

_____

_____

_____

_____

_____

_____

_____

_____

_____

_____

Ideas Teammates Share

United States Social Studies: Engaging Cooperative Learning Activities
Kagan Publishing • 800.933.2667 • www.KaganOnline.com

Formation of a New Government
Judicial Branch

Directions: Think about the prompt, and then write your own response. When done, RoundRobin share your writing with your teammates. Use the space at the bottom to record ideas your teammates share.

Prompt

Imagine the United States without a judicial branch. How would life be different if this branch did not exist?

My Writing

_____

_____

_____

_____

_____

_____

_____

_____

_____

_____

_____

Ideas Teammates Share

United States Social Studies: Engaging Cooperative Learning Activities
Kagan Publishing • 800.933.2667 • www.KaganOnline.com

95

Formation of a New Government
Executive Branch

Directions: Think about the prompt, and then write your own response. When done, RoundRobin share your writing with your teammates. Use the space at the bottom to record ideas your teammates share.

Prompt

Imagine that you are asked to visit the White House to act as a student adviser to the president. What advice would you offer? Explain your thinking.

My Writing

_____

_____

_____

_____

_____

_____

_____

_____

_____

_____

_____

_____

Ideas Teammates Share

United States Social Studies: Engaging Cooperative Learning Activities
Kagan Publishing • 800.933.2667 • www.KaganOnline.com

Formation of a New Government
Executive Branch

Directions: Think about the prompt, and then write your own response. When done, RoundRobin share your writing with your teammates. Use the space at the bottom to record ideas your teammates share.

Prompt

You have been given the opportunity to interview a member of the executive branch of the government and you may only ask one question. Who would you interview? What is the one question you would ask? Explain your reasoning.

My Writing

_____

_____

_____

_____

_____

_____

_____

_____

_____

_____

Ideas Teammates Share

United States Social Studies: Engaging Cooperative Learning Activities
Kagan Publishing • 800.933.2667 • www.KaganOnline.com

97

Formation of a New Government
Checks and Balances System

Directions: Think about the prompt, and then write your own response. When done, RoundRobin share your writing with your teammates. Use the space at the bottom to record ideas your teammates share.

Prompt

Describe the importance of our government's Checks and Balances system. How would our world be different if this system did not exist?

My Writing

_____

_____

_____

_____

_____

_____

_____

_____

_____

_____

_____

Ideas Teammates Share

United States Social Studies: Engaging Cooperative Learning Activities
Kagan Publishing • 800.933.2667 • www.KaganOnline.com

Formation of a New Government
A New Government

Directions: Think about the prompt, and then write your own response. When done, RoundRobin share your writing with your teammates. Use the space at the bottom to record ideas your teammates share.

Prompt

Imagine you are a nationalist following the Revolutionary War. Write a speech arguing for a new, stronger government using events and facts to support your position.

My Writing

_____

_____

_____

_____

_____

_____

_____

_____

_____

_____

_____

_____

Ideas Teammates Share

United States Social Studies: Engaging Cooperative Learning Activities
Kagan Publishing • 800.933.2667 • www.KaganOnline.com

99

Formation of a New Government
Legislative Branch

■ **RallyCoach Directions:** Take turns answering each question as your partner coaches. Explain your thinking to your coach.
■ **Sage-N-Scribe Directions:** The Sage describes what he or she knows about the question so the Scribe can answer the question. The Sage and Scribe switch roles for each question.

Name _____

1. Which of the following is NOT part of the legislative branch?
   a) President
   b) House of Representatives
   c) Congress
   d) Senate

2. How long does each Congress last?
   a) 4 years
   b) 5 years
   c) 2 years
   d) 6 years

3. How many representatives serve each state in the House of Representatives?
   a) Two representatives
   b) Depends on the size of the state
   c) 435 representatives
   d) Depends on number of people in the state

4. Which of the following is NOT a requirement to serve as a state representative?
   a) Serve in the military
   b) Be at least 25 years old
   c) Be a United States citizen for the past 7 years
   d) Live in the state they represent

5. How long is the term for a senator?
   a) 4 years
   b) 6 years
   c) 3 years
   d) Unlimited

Name _____

1. What is the purpose of the legislative branch?
   a) To make our laws
   b) To enforce our laws
   c) To interpret our laws
   d) To police our laws

2. Which two parts make up the Congress?
   a) The House of Representatives and Pentagon
   b) The Senate and Vice President
   c) The President and Secretary of State
   d) The House of Representatives and Senate

3. How long is the term for a state representative?
   a) 4 years
   b) 2 years
   c) 3 years
   d) 6 years

4. How many senators represent each state?
   a) Depends on how large a state is
   b) Six senators
   c) Depends on how many people live in that state
   d) Two senators

5. Which of the following is NOT a requirement to be a senator?
   a) Be at least 30 years old
   b) Live in the state he or she represents
   c) Be a U.S. citizen for the past 9 years
   d) Be born in the state he or she represents

United States Social Studies: Engaging Cooperative Learning Activities
Kagan Publishing • 800.933.2667 • www.KaganOnline.com

Formation of a New Government

The Amendments to the Constitution

- **RallyCoach Directions:** Take turns answering each question as your partner coaches. Explain your thinking to your coach.
- **Sage-N-Scribe Directions:** The Sage describes what he or she knows about the question so the Scribe can answer the question. The Sage and Scribe switch roles for each question.

Name _____

1. What does the Fourth Amendment protect against?
   a) Law against freedom of speech
   b) Law against freedom of religion
   c) Cruel and unusual punishment
   d) Unlawful search and seizure

2. What right is guaranteed in the Sixth Amendment?
   a) Freedom of speech
   b) Right to a fair and speedy trial
   c) Citizens over age 18 having the right to vote
   d) Right to bear arms

3. What does the Tenth Amendment state?
   a) Slavery is not allowed in the United States.
   b) Powers not given to the federal government in the Constitution belong to the state or to the people.
   c) Citizens have the right to a fair and speedy trial.
   d) U.S. citizens over the age of 18 are allowed to vote.

4. Carter is able to have a job, earn a paycheck for his work, pay taxes, and make his own decisions. He is not forced to work for anyone else. His ancestors fought for these freedoms in the Civil War. What amendment protects this right?
   a) First Amendment
   b) Second Amendment
   c) Twelfth Amendment
   d) Thirteenth Amendment

5. Billy disagrees with a new policy at his school and decides to write his opinion for the school newspaper to publish and distribute to other students. Which amendment protects this right?
   a) First Amendment
   b) Second Amendment
   c) Sixth Amendment
   d) Twenty-Sixth Amendment

Name _____

1. Which amendment states that a person cannot be tried for a serious crime unless accused by a grand jury; a person cannot be forced to testify against himself; and paid-for property may not be taken for public use?
   a) Fifth Amendment
   b) Sixth Amendment
   c) Tenth Amendment
   d) Thirteenth Amendment

2. Which of the following is not prohibited by the protections of the Eighth Amendment?
   a) Excessive or high bail
   b) Cruel and unusual punishment
   c) Death penalty
   d) Stiff fines

3. What right is given in the Nineteenth Amendment?
   a) Women are given the right to vote.
   b) Powers not given to the federal government in the Constitution belong to the state or to the people.
   c) Citizens over age 21 are given the right to vote.
   d) Right to a fair and speedy trial.

4. Roger keeps a rifle in his home to use during hunting season. His right to own the gun is protected by what amendment in the Bill of Rights?
   a) Fourth Amendment
   b) Eighth Amendment
   c) Second Amendment
   d) First Amendment

5. Lynn just celebrated her 18th birthday. Which amendment now allows her the right to vote?
   a) Sixth Amendment
   b) Fifteenth Amendment
   c) Nineteenth Amendment
   d) Twenty-sixth Amendment

United States Social Studies: Engaging Cooperative Learning Activities
Kagan Publishing • 800.933.2667 • www.KaganOnline.com

101

Formation of a New Government
The Amendments to the Constitution

Directions: Copy one set of cards for each team. Cut out each card along the dotted lines. Give each team a set of cards to play Fan-N-Pick or Showdown.

1
Formation of a New Government

What right is given in the Twenty-Sixth Amendment?

Fan-N-Pick/Showdown

2
Formation of a New Government

What right is protected in the Second Amendment?

Fan-N-Pick/Showdown

3
Formation of a New Government

Which amendment states that the government cannot force citizens to provide shelter to soldiers in their home?

Fan-N-Pick/Showdown

4
Formation of a New Government

What right does the Seventh Amendment give to U.S. citizens?

Fan-N-Pick/Showdown

5
Formation of a New Government

Explain what the Ninth Amendment says about the rights of citizens.

Fan-N-Pick/Showdown

6
Formation of a New Government

What is barred by the Thirteenth Amendment?

Fan-N-Pick/Showdown

7
Formation of a New Government

List the five freedoms protected by the First Amendment.

Fan-N-Pick/Showdown

8
Formation of a New Government

Sally Sloan, a female teacher, casts her vote in the election of the president. Which amendment protects her right to do this?

Fan-N-Pick/Showdown

9
Formation of a New Government

A police officer knocks on the door of Gary's house asking to search his home for evidence in a recent robbery. Which amendment protects Gary's right to refuse to give the officer permission to enter?

Fan-N-Pick/Showdown

10
Formation of a New Government

Which amendment determines the number of successive terms a president can be elected?

Fan-N-Pick/Showdown

Formation of a New Government
The New America

Directions: Cut out each card along the dotted lines. Then fold each card in half so the question is on one side and the answer is on the back. Glue or tape the cards together to keep the answers and questions on opposite sides.

---

1 Formation of a New Government

Which of the following was a result of the new American government's inability to collect taxes?

a) Soldiers of the Revolutionary War could not be paid.
b) The American government was unable to appoint a leader.
c) There were multiple versions of printed and coined money.
d) Borrowed money or debts, were paid in full following the war.

Quiz-Quiz-Trade • Question

---

1 Formation of a New Government

Which of the following was a result of the new American government's inability to collect taxes?

a) Soldiers of the Revolutionary War could not be paid.

Quiz-Quiz-Trade • Answer

---

2 Formation of a New Government

Which is true about the currency in America following the Revolutionary War?

a) Citizens primarily used printed money from Britain.
b) Congress and states had the ability to print their own money.
c) The federal government printed standard money for the new country.
d) Congresses' printed money was worth more than state money.

Quiz-Quiz-Trade • Question

---

2 Formation of a New Government

Which is true about the currency in America following the Revolutionary War?

b) Congress and states had the ability to print their own money.

Quiz-Quiz-Trade • Answer

---

3 Formation of a New Government

What was the Nationalist viewpoint in the 1780s?

a) They felt the government was weak and should return to British rule.
b) They felt the government was strong and should continue to limit national involvement.
c) They felt the nation needed a newer, stronger national government.
d) They felt the nation needed a government who did not deal with other nations.

Quiz-Quiz-Trade • Question

---

3 Formation of a New Government

What was the viewpoint of a nationalist in the 1780s?

c) They felt the nation needed a newer, stronger national government.

Quiz-Quiz-Trade • Answer

United States Social Studies: Engaging Cooperative Learning Activities
Kagan Publishing • 800.933.2667 • www.KaganOnline.com

103

Formation of a New Government
The New America

Directions: Cut out each card along the dotted lines. Then fold each card in half so the question is on one side and the answer is on the back. Glue or tape the cards together to keep the answers and questions on opposite sides.

---

④ Formation of a New Government

What was the cause of Shay's Rebellion in Massachusetts?

a) The government demanded a piece of farm profits.
b) The farmers demanded help from the government after their crops were destroyed during the Revolutionary War.
c) The government split up farm territories for former slaves to live and work.
d) The farmers were being forced to pay high taxes to repay debts from the war, and if they could not pay, they were jailed.

Quiz-Quiz-Trade • Question

---

④ Formation of a New Government

What was the cause of Shay's Rebellion in Massachusetts?

d) The farmers were being forced to pay high taxes to repay debts from the war, and if they could not pay, they were jailed.

Quiz-Quiz-Trade • Answer

---

⑤ Formation of a New Government

Which of the following was not part of the Northwest Ordinance of 1787?

a) Prohibiting the use of slaves
b) Peace treaties with American Indians
c) Freedom of speech and religion
d) Establishment of public schools

Quiz-Quiz-Trade • Question

---

⑤ Formation of a New Government

Which of the following was not part of the Northwest Ordinance?

b) Peace treaties with American Indians

Quiz-Quiz-Trade • Answer

---

⑥ Formation of a New Government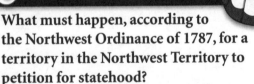

What must happen, according to the Northwest Ordinance of 1787, for a territory in the Northwest Territory to petition for statehood?

a) Sustain citizenship for a minimum of 5 years
b) Cut all ties to former British
c) The "new" state must pledge to remain beneath the power of the original 13 states
d) The adult male population must reach 60,000

Quiz-Quiz-Trade • Question

---

⑥ Formation of a New Government

What must happen, according to the Northwest Ordinance of 1787, for a territory in the Northwest Territory to petition for statehood?

d) The adult male population must reach 60,000

Quiz-Quiz-Trade • Answer

104

United States Social Studies: Engaging Cooperative Learning Activities
Kagan Publishing • 800.933.2667 • www.KaganOnline.com

Formation of a New Government
The New America

Directions: Cut out each card along the dotted lines. Then fold each card in half so the question is on one side and the answer is on the back. Glue or tape the cards together to keep the answers and questions on opposite sides.

---

7 Formation of a New Government

Where was the Constitutional Convention held?

a) Philadelphia, Pennsylvania
b) Richmond, Virginia
c) Washington, D.C.
d) Boston, Massachusetts

Quiz-Quiz-Trade • Question

---

7 Formation of a New Government

Where was the Constitutional Convention held?

a) Philadelphia, Pennsylvania

Quiz-Quiz-Trade • Answer

---

8 Formation of a New Government

Who was unanimously voted to lead the Constitutional Convention?

a) James Madison
b) Benjamin Franklin
c) Alexander Hamilton
d) George Washington

Quiz-Quiz-Trade • Question

---

8 Formation of a New Government

Who was unanimously voted to lead the Constitutional Convention?

d) George Washington

Quiz-Quiz-Trade • Answer

---

9 Formation of a New Government

Which of the following statements is NOT true regarding the Constitutional Convention?

a) Guards were placed outside the doors to keep the meeting secret.
b) The windows of the meeting hall were nailed shut.
c) The convention was during winter months and very cold during discussions.
d) James Madison kept day-to-day notes of the discussion.

Quiz-Quiz-Trade • Question

---

9 Formation of a New Government

Which of the following statements is NOT true regarding the Constitutional Convention?

c) The convention was during winter months and very cold during discussions.

Quiz-Quiz-Trade • Answer

United States Social Studies: Engaging Cooperative Learning Activities
Kagan Publishing • 800.933.2667 • www.KaganOnline.com

105

Formation of a New Government
The New America

Directions: Cut out each card along the dotted lines. Then fold each card in half so the question is on one side and the answer is on the back. Glue or tape the cards together to keep the answers and questions on opposite sides.

---

10 Formation of a New Government

Which sentence best summarizes the Virginia Plan?

a) Larger states should have more representation in government than smaller states because they cover more land area.
b) Congress will be given greater power over states with an executive branch to carry out laws and a judicial branch to interpret laws.
c) All states should be equal in representation, regardless of size of population.
d) Congress should delegate all responsibilities and decision making to larger states.

Quiz-Quiz-Trade • Question

---

10 Formation of a New Government

Which sentence best summarizes the Virginia Plan?

b) Congress will be given greater power over states with an executive branch to carry out laws and a judicial branch to interpret laws.

Quiz-Quiz-Trade • Answer

---

11 Formation of a New Government

What was the name of the plan, proposed by delegate William Paterson, which suggested each state have equal representation in Congress?

a) Articles of Confederation
b) The Compromise Plan
c) Virginia Plan
d) New Jersey Plan

Quiz-Quiz-Trade • Question

---

11 Formation of a New Government

What was the name of the plan, proposed by delegate William Paterson, which suggested each state have equal representation in Congress?

d) New Jersey Plan

Quiz-Quiz-Trade • Answer

---

12 Formation of a New Government

How did the Great Compromise shape Congress?

a) There is a House of Representatives where population determines representatives and the Senate determines equal representation from states.
b) States with larger land size will have more representation in the House of Representatives but equal in the Senate.
c) The House of Representatives and Senate will be equal in state representation.
d) The original 13 Colonies will have greater representation in the Senate than in the House of Representatives.

Quiz-Quiz-Trade • Question

---

12 Formation of a New Government

How did the Great Compromise shape Congress?

a) There is a House of Representatives where population determines representatives and the Senate determines equal representation from states.

Quiz-Quiz-Trade • Answer

United States Social Studies: Engaging Cooperative Learning Activities
Kagan Publishing • 800.933.2667 • www.KaganOnline.com

Formation of a New Government
The New America

Directions: Cut out each card along the dotted lines. Then fold each card in half so the question is on one side and the answer is on the back. Glue or tape the cards together to keep the answers and questions on opposite sides.

---

13 Formation of a New Government

What was the Three-Fifths Compromise?

a) Three-fifths of the House of Representatives must be made up of representatives from the 13 Colonies.
b) Three-fifths of the slave population would remain enslaved and count, but the remaining two-fifths would be freed.
c) Three-fifths of the slave population would count for representation and taxes.
d) Three-fifths of each population would count towards the House of Representatives.

Quiz-Quiz-Trade • Question

---

13 Formation of a New Government

What was the Three-Fifths Compromise?

c) Three-fifths of the slave population would count for representation and taxes.

Quiz-Quiz-Trade • Answer

---

14 Formation of a New Government

Which of the following is NOT stated in the preamble to the Constitution as a goal?

a) Establish justice
b) Defend the nation
c) Protect people's well-being and liberty
d) Promise quality leadership

Quiz-Quiz-Trade • Question

---

14 Formation of a New Government

Which of the following is NOT stated in the preamble as a goal of the Constitution?

d) Promise quality leadership

Quiz-Quiz-Trade • Answer

---

15 Formation of a New Government

Which of the following is a reserved power, a power left for the state to decide?

a) Making laws about trading with other countries
b) Managing public education
c) Producing coins and paper money
d) Defending the nation with a military

Quiz-Quiz-Trade • Question

---

15 Formation of a New Government

Which of the following is a reserved power, a power left for the state to decide?

b) Managing public education

Quiz-Quiz-Trade • Answer

United States Social Studies: Engaging Cooperative Learning Activities
Kagan Publishing • 800.933.2667 • www.KaganOnline.com

107

Formation of a New Government
Executive Branch

Name: _____

Directions: Pair up and take turns answering each question. Don't forget to get your partner's initials.

① What is the primary purpose of the executive branch?

_____
_____
_____
_____

_____ Initials

② Who is the leader of the country and the commander in chief of the military?

_____
_____
_____
_____

_____ Initials

③ What is the role of the vice president?

_____
_____
_____
_____

_____ Initials

④ What is the purpose of the department heads, also known as cabinet members?

_____
_____
_____
_____

_____ Initials

⑤ What is the purpose of the Presidential Succession Act of 1947?

_____
_____
_____
_____

_____ Initials

⑥ How old does a president need to be in order to serve?

_____
_____
_____
_____

_____ Initials

⑦ Name three presidents who have served in the executive branch?

_____
_____
_____
_____

_____ Initials

⑧ If the president, vice president, and the president pro tempore of the Senate are unable to serve office, who will take over the presidency?

_____
_____
_____

_____ Initials

⑨ Who is our current President of the United States?

_____
_____
_____
_____

_____ Initials

United States Social Studies: Engaging Cooperative Learning Activities
Kagan Publishing • 800.933.2667 • www.KaganOnline.com

108

Formation of a New Government

Branches of Government

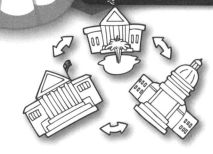

Name: _____

Directions: Pair up and take turns answering each question. Don't forget to get your partner's initials.

1 Which branch of government makes sure laws are carried out?

_____
_____
_____
_____

_____ Initials

2 Which branch of government establishes taxes?

_____
_____
_____
_____

_____ Initials

3 Which branch of government is responsible for deciding if new laws are constitutional?

_____
_____
_____
_____

_____ Initials

4 Who is the head of the executive branch?

_____
_____
_____
_____

_____ Initials

5 What must Congress do in order to override a president's veto?

_____
_____
_____
_____

_____ Initials

6 Which branch does the Supreme Court belong to?

_____
_____
_____
_____

_____ Initials

7 Which branch is responsible for making laws?

_____
_____
_____
_____

_____ Initials

8 Which branch interprets the laws of our nation?

_____
_____
_____
_____

_____ Initials

9 What term is given to the system of making sure each branch of government has equal power?

_____
_____
_____
_____

_____ Initials

United States Social Studies: Engaging Cooperative Learning Activities
Kagan Publishing • 800.933.2667 • www.KaganOnline.com

109

Formation of a New Government
Branches of Government

Name: _____

Directions: Pair up and take turns answering each question. Don't forget to get your partner's initials.

① What branch of government is responsible for making laws?

_____

_____

Initials

② Which branch of government includes the House of Representatives and the Senate?

_____

_____

Initials

③ Who wrote "The Star-Spangled Banner"?

_____

_____

Initials

④ What are the three branches of government?

_____

_____

Initials

⑤ What historic document lists America's protected freedoms?

_____

_____

Initials

⑥ Which branch of government is made up of the court system?

_____

_____

Initials

⑦ How many states are there currently in our nation?

_____

_____

Initials

⑧ Which historic document was written as the first step toward separation from Great Britain?

_____

_____

Initials

⑨ What is the current Capitol of the United States of America?

_____

_____

Initials

⑩ Which color of the flag signifies valor and bravery?

_____

_____

Initials

⑪ Which branch of government does the vice president belong to?

_____

_____

Initials

⑫ Which branch of government has veto power?

_____

_____

Initials

United States Social Studies: Engaging Cooperative Learning Activities
Kagan Publishing • 800.933.2667 • www.KaganOnline.com

110

Westward Expansion

Cooperative Learning Activities

Westward Expansion
The Homestead Act

Directions: Think about the prompt, and then write your own response. When done, RoundRobin share your writing with your teammates. Use the space at the bottom to record ideas your teammates share.

Prompt: Imagine you live in 1862 and have just read about the Homestead Act in the newspaper. You meet the requirements to own your own land. Would you move your family for the opportunity of the Homestead Act or not? Explain your thinking.

My writing: _____

_____

_____

_____

_____

_____

_____

_____

_____

_____

Ideas Teammates Share

112

United States Social Studies: Engaging Cooperative Learning Activities
Kagan Publishing • 800.933.2667 • www.KaganOnline.com

Westward Expansion
The Pony Express

Directions: Think about the prompt, and then write your own response. When done, RoundRobin share your writing with your teammates. Use the space at the bottom to record ideas your teammates share.

Prompt: Would you have wanted to be a rider for the Pony Express? Explain your thinking using details from history.

My writing: _____

_____

_____

_____

_____

_____

_____

_____

_____

_____

_____

Ideas Teammates Share

United States Social Studies: Engaging Cooperative Learning Activities
Kagan Publishing • 800.933.2667 • www.KaganOnline.com

113

Westward Expansion
The Pony Express

Directions: Think about the prompt, and then write your own response. When done, RoundRobin share your writing with your teammates. Use the space at the bottom to record ideas your teammates share.

Prompt: In your opinion, what was the most dangerous part of being a rider for the Pony Express? Justify your thinking using details from history.

My writing: _____

_____

_____

_____

_____

_____

_____

_____

_____

_____

Ideas Teammates Share

United States Social Studies: Engaging Cooperative Learning Activities
Kagan Publishing • 800.933.2667 • www.KaganOnline.com

Westward Expansion
The Pony Express

Directions: Think about the prompt, and then write your own response. When done, RoundRobin share your writing with your teammates. Use the space at the bottom to record ideas your teammates share.

Prompt: What impact did the Pony Express have on history and those living during that period? Explain your thinking.

My writing: _____

_____

_____

_____

_____

_____

_____

_____

_____

_____

_____

_____

Ideas Teammates Share

United States Social Studies: Engaging Cooperative Learning Activities
Kagan Publishing • 800.933.2667 • www.KaganOnline.com

115

Westward Expansion
The Pony Express

■ **RallyCoach Directions:** Take turns answering each question as your partner coaches. Explain your thinking to your coach.

■ **Sage-N-Scribe Directions:** The Sage describes what he or she knows about the question so the Scribe can answer the question. The Sage and Scribe switch roles for each question.

Name _____

1. Where did the Pony Express begin its route?
   a) San Diego, California
   b) Saint Joseph, Missouri
   c) Pittsburg, Kansas
   d) Omaha, Nebraska

2. What was the main purpose of the Pony Express?
   a) To deliver mail in a shortened amount of time
   b) To bring new settlers across the west
   c) To have protection for the families heading west
   d) To search for gold routes heading to California

3. Which of the following is NOT considered a danger of the trail?
   a) Frostbite
   b) Dehydration
   c) Heat exhaustion
   d) Animal attacks

4. Who eventually won the mail contract?
   a) Samuel Morse
   b) The Pony Express
   c) Overland Stage Company
   d) The Morning Transcript

5. When did the Pony Express officially stop its service?
   a) December 1860
   b) October 1861
   c) January 1862
   d) August 1901

Name _____

1. When did the Pony Express begin?
   a) July 1890
   b) January 1954
   c) August 1690
   d) January 1860

2. Why did the riders wear a red shirt and blue pants?
   a) To identify them as American riders
   b) As a sign of friendly people towards the tribes
   c) To be seen easily from a distance
   d) As a way to represent the change of America

3. What invention, created in 1844 by Samuel F. B. Morse, made communication faster?
   a) Steam train
   b) Telegraph
   c) Mail wagons
   d) Telephone

4. Approximately how many men rode for the Pony Express during its short time?
   a) Over 500
   b) Around 250
   c) Less than 100
   d) No more than 175

5. What is one reason the politicians wanted to use stage coaches for mail transportation?
   a) They were faster than horses.
   b) Fewer men could be used and thus paid.
   c) The stagecoaches were safer from attacks.
   d) The coaches could carry magazines and packages.

United States Social Studies: Engaging Cooperative Learning Activities
Kagan Publishing • 800.933.2667 • www.KaganOnline.com

Westward Expansion
The Monroe Doctrine

■ **RallyCoach Directions:** Take turns answering each question as your partner coaches. Explain your thinking to your coach.
■ **Sage-N-Scribe Directions:** The Sage describes what he or she knows about the question so the Scribe can answer the question. The Sage and Scribe switch roles for each question.

Name _____

1. Newly elected President James Monroe believed in Nationalism. What is Nationalism?
   a) Belief that all people should come together with pride in their country
   b) The federal government is important above all else.
   c) The national system is dependent solely on its leaders.
   d) A nation cannot survive without its wars.

2. Who did President Monroe send to defend American settlements from raids by American Indians?
   a) He went himself.
   b) James Madison
   c) Benjamin Franklin
   d) Andrew Jackson

3. How much did America pay for the Florida Territory?
   a) $10 million
   b) $2 million
   c) $5 million
   d) $8 million

Name _____

1. What was the purpose of the Monroe's statement, the Monroe Doctrine?
   a) Settle a peace treaty for land south of Georgia
   b) Warn European countries against interfering with America
   c) Remove American Indians from Eastern settlements
   d) Provide peace among American Indians and settlers

2. Why did Spain finally decide to sell Florida to America?
   a) Spain had trouble defending Florida.
   b) American Indians chose to side with American troops.
   c) Escaped slaves were moving from Georgia into Florida.
   d) France signed a treaty with America for more troops.

3. What other countries were interested in taking over the Spanish's weakened territories in America?
   a) Argentina and Mexico
   b) Russia and Britain
   c) France and Portugal
   d) Scotland and the West Indies

United States Social Studies: Engaging Cooperative Learning Activities
Kagan Publishing • 800.933.2667 • www.KaganOnline.com

117

Westward Expansion
The Lewis and Clark Expedition

■ **RallyCoach Directions:** Take turns answering each question as your partner coaches. Explain your thinking to your coach.
■ **Sage-N-Scribe Directions:** The Sage describes what he or she knows about the question so the Scribe can answer the question. The Sage and Scribe switch roles for each question.

Name _____

1. Who asked Meriwether Lewis and William Clark to explore the newly purchased Louisiana Territory?
a) President Thomas Jefferson
b) Sacagawea and Toussaint Charbonneau
c) Vice President Aaron Burr
d) Seaman

2. What is one reason Lewis and Clark wanted Sacagawea to accompany them on their expedition?
a) She was able to translate many American Indian languages.
b) She was a wonderful cook.
c) She wanted to return home to France.
d) She could help trade with American Indians.

3. Which tribe did Sacagawea belong to?
a) Oto
b) Shoshone
c) Hidatsa
d) Nez Perce

4. How many modern day states were a part of the Louisiana Purchase?
a) 16
b) 50
c) 9
d) 15

5. Which of the following is a reason the American government wanted the Louisiana Territory?
a) To protect gold found in California
b) To see if there were any unknown animals
c) The east was getting crowded and the territory would double America's size.
d) To set up trade agreements with American Indians

Name _____

1. What was the name of the group of men that traveled with Meriwether Lewis and William Clark?
a) Lewis and Clark Journeymen
b) Expedition Explorers
c) Corps of Discovery
d) Peace Corps

2. After the winter at Fort Mandan, why did the captains order a boat of men back to St. Louis?
a) To update President Jefferson about the journey so far
b) To return the wounded to their families
c) To create a safe passage back home
d) To gather new supplies and ammunition

3. Who did the United States purchase the Louisiana Territory from for $15 million?
a) Great Britain
b) France
c) Spain
d) Mexico

4. About how long did the Corps of Discovery expedition take?
a) More than 2 years
b) Less than 16 months
c) Just under 4 years
d) Twenty-one months and 3 days

5. Why did Lewis and Clark hire French-Canadian fur trader Toussaint Charbonneau?
a) He lead the Corps of Discovery through the Rocky mountains.
b) He could act as a translator.
c) He was an excellent fisherman.
d) He was very interested in the wildlife.

118

United States Social Studies: Engaging Cooperative Learning Activities
Kagan Publishing • 800.933.2667 • www.KaganOnline.com

Westward Expansion
The Indian Removal Act / Trail of Tears

Directions: Copy one set of cards for each team. Cut out each card along the dotted lines. Give each team a set of cards to play Fan-N-Pick or Showdown.

---

1 · *Westward Expansion*

Name three of the five major American Indian tribes of the Southeast in which settlers moved into their land.

Fan-N-Pick/Showdown

---

2 · *Westward Expansion*

What was the name of the act President Jackson passed that allowed the moving of American Indians?

Fan-N-Pick/Showdown

---

3 · *Westward Expansion*

What was the purpose of the Indian Removal Act?

Fan-N-Pick/Showdown

---

4 · *Westward Expansion*

Using present-day geography, where were the American Indians moved to following the Indian Removal Act?

Fan-N-Pick/Showdown

---

5 · *Westward Expansion*

Which American Indian tribe, led by John Ross, tried to take their case to the Supreme Court in order to stay in Georgia?

Fan-N-Pick/Showdown

---

6 · *Westward Expansion*

In 1838, which president ordered the forceful removal of Cherokee Indians from their land?

Fan-N-Pick/Showdown

---

7 · *Westward Expansion*

Approximately how many Cherokee Indians were forced to leave their homes in 1838?

Fan-N-Pick/Showdown

---

8 · *Westward Expansion*

What did the 800-mile journey become known as when the American Indians were forced to take to new territory?

Fan-N-Pick/Showdown

United States Social Studies: Engaging Cooperative Learning Activities
Kagan Publishing • 800.933.2667 • www.KaganOnline.com

119

Westward Expansion
The Louisiana Purchase

Directions: Copy one set of cards for each team. Cut out each card along the dotted lines. Give each team a set of cards to play Fan-N-Pick or Showdown.

---

1 *Westward Expansion*

Who was president during the Louisiana Purchase?

Fan-N-Pick/Showdown

---

2 *Westward Expansion*

What caused President Jefferson to seek purchase of the Louisiana Territory?

Fan-N-Pick/Showdown

---

3 *Westward Expansion*

Who did President Jefferson send to negotiate the purchase of the Louisiana Territory?

Fan-N-Pick/Showdown

---

4 *Westward Expansion*

What country owned the Louisiana Territory?

Fan-N-Pick/Showdown

---

5 *Westward Expansion*

Who was the Emperor of France who negotiated the sale of the Louisiana Territory?

Fan-N-Pick/Showdown

---

6 *Westward Expansion*

In what year was the Louisiana Purchase complete?

Fan-N-Pick/Showdown

---

7 *Westward Expansion*

What was the final price of the Louisiana Purchase?

Fan-N-Pick/Showdown

---

8 *Westward Expansion*

What happened to the land size of America after the Louisiana Purchase?

Fan-N-Pick/Showdown

---

9 *Westward Expansion*

What caused Napoleon to change his mind and sell the Louisiana Territory to America?

Fan-N-Pick/Showdown

---

10 *Westward Expansion*

What port in the Louisiana Territory was important to exports of American goods?

Fan-N-Pick/Showdown

120

United States Social Studies: Engaging Cooperative Learning Activities
Kagan Publishing • 800.933.2667 • www.KaganOnline.com

Westward Expansion
The Lewis and Clark Expedition

Directions: Cut out each card along the dotted lines. Then fold each card in half so the question is on one side and the answer is on the back. Glue or tape the cards together to keep the answers and questions on opposite sides.

1 *Westward Expansion*

Which president requested Captains Meriwether Lewis and William Clark to explore the Louisiana Territory?

Quiz-Quiz-Trade • Question

1 *Westward Expansion*

Which president requested Captains Meriwether Lewis and William Clark to explore the Louisiana Territory?
President Thomas Jefferson

Quiz-Quiz-Trade • Answer

2 *Westward Expansion*

The United States paid the _____ $15 million for the Louisiana Territory.

Quiz-Quiz-Trade • Question

2 *Westward Expansion*

The United States paid the _____ $15 million for the Louisiana Territory.
French

Quiz-Quiz-Trade • Answer

3 *Westward Expansion*

What is the name given to the sale of the Louisiana Territory from the French to the United States?

Quiz-Quiz-Trade • Question

3 *Westward Expansion*

What is the name given to the sale of the Louisiana Territory from the French to the United States?
Louisiana Purchase

Quiz-Quiz-Trade • Answer

4 *Westward Expansion*

What did Lewis and Clark call the group of men joining their journey?

Quiz-Quiz-Trade • Question

4 *Westward Expansion*

What did Lewis and Clark call the group of men joining their journey?
Corps (KOR) of Discovery

Quiz-Quiz-Trade • Answer

***United States Social Studies:* Engaging Cooperative Learning Activities**
Kagan Publishing • 800.933.2667 • www.KaganOnline.com

121

Westward Expansion
The Lewis and Clark Expedition

Directions: Cut out each card along the dotted lines. Then fold each card in half so the question is on one side and the answer is on the back. Glue or tape the cards together to keep the answers and questions on opposite sides.

---

5 *Westward Expansion*

True or False: Lewis and Clark were able to use accurate maps to help them on their journey.

Quiz-Quiz-Trade • Question

---

5 *Westward Expansion*

True or False: Lewis and Clark were able to use accurate maps to help them on their journey.

False: Lewis and Clark made their own maps during the journey because it was new, uncharted territory.

Quiz-Quiz-Trade • Answer

---

6 *Westward Expansion*

Name at least three items the Corps of Discovery took with them on their journey.

Quiz-Quiz-Trade • Question

---

6 *Westward Expansion*

Name at least three items the Corps of Discovery took with them on their journey.

Any 3: food, muskets, knives, a compass, and a dog named Seaman.

Quiz-Quiz-Trade • Answer

---

7 *Westward Expansion*

How did the corps navigate the difficult route upstream against the Missouri River's current?

Quiz-Quiz-Trade • Question

---

7 *Westward Expansion*

How did the corps navigate the difficult route upstream against the Missouri River's current?

The men rowed or used long poles to push off from the river bottom.

Quiz-Quiz-Trade • Answer

---

8 *Westward Expansion*

How did Lewis try to make friends with the American Indians he met during his journey?

Quiz-Quiz-Trade • Question

---

8 *Westward Expansion*

How did Lewis try to make friends with the American Indians he meet during his journey?

Lewis gave them gifts such as fishhooks, knives, and blankets.

Quiz-Quiz-Trade • Answer

United States Social Studies: Engaging Cooperative Learning Activities
Kagan Publishing • 800.933.2667 • www.KaganOnline.com

122

Westward Expansion
The Lewis and Clark Expedition

Directions: Cut out each card along the dotted lines. Then fold each card in half so the question is on one side and the answer is on the back. Glue or tape the cards together to keep the answers and questions on opposite sides.

9
Westward Expansion

What caused the Corps of Discovery to build Fort Mandan and spend 5 months with the Mandan?

Quiz-Quiz-Trade • Question

9
Westward Expansion

What caused the Corps of Discovery to build Fort Mandan and spend 5 months with the Mandan?

Winter was coming and travel on the frozen Missouri River would be difficult.

Quiz-Quiz-Trade • Answer

10
Westward Expansion

Lewis and Clark hired French-Canadian fur trader Toussain Charbonneau (too-SAUN shar-bone-Oh) to be an _____.

Quiz-Quiz-Trade • Question

10
Westward Expansion

Lewis and Clark hired French-Canadian fur trader Toussain Charbonneau (too-SAUN shar-bone-Oh) to be an _____.

interpreter

Quiz-Quiz-Trade • Answer

11
Westward Expansion

In addition to exploring land, Lewis and Clark documented _____ and _____ never seen before in the east.

Quiz-Quiz-Trade • Question

11
Westward Expansion

In addition to exploring land, Lewis and Clark documented _____ and _____ never seen before in the east.

animals, plants

Quiz-Quiz-Trade • Answer

12
Westward Expansion

How did the corps get around the Great Falls of the Missouri River?

Quiz-Quiz-Trade • Question

12
Westward Expansion

How did the corps get around the Great Falls of the Missouri River?

The men built wagons to carry their supplies around the falls.

Quiz-Quiz-Trade • Answer

United States Social Studies: Engaging Cooperative Learning Activities
Kagan Publishing • 800.933.2667 • www.KaganOnline.com

123

Westward Expansion
The Lewis and Clark Expedition

Directions: Cut out each card along the dotted lines. Then fold each card in half so the question is on one side and the answer is on the back. Glue or tape the cards together to keep the answers and questions on opposite sides.

13 *Westward Expansion*

In July 1805, nearly 1 year after the journey began, Meriwether Lewis got his first view of the _____ _____.

Quiz-Quiz-Trade • Question

13 *Westward Expansion*

In July 1805, nearly 1 year after the journey began, Meriwether Lewis got his first view of the _____ _____.

Rocky Mountains

Quiz-Quiz-Trade • Answer

14 *Westward Expansion*

How did Sacagawea help the corps cross the Rocky Mountains?

Quiz-Quiz-Trade • Question

14 *Westward Expansion*

How did Sacagawea help the corps cross the Rocky Mountains?

She convinced the Shoshone (show-SHOW-nee) to assist the men with finding a route through the mountains.

Quiz-Quiz-Trade • Answer

15 *Westward Expansion*

The Nez Perce (NEZ PURSE) gave Lewis and his men _____ to eat and the root of a plant called _____.

Quiz-Quiz-Trade • Question

15 *Westward Expansion*

The Nez Perce (NEZ PURSE) gave Lewis and his men _____ to eat and the root of a plant called _____.

salmon, camas (KAM-uhs)

Quiz-Quiz-Trade • Answer

16 *Westward Expansion*

How did the men of the Corps of Discovery celebrate reaching the shore of the Pacific Ocean?

Quiz-Quiz-Trade • Question

16 *Westward Expansion*

How did the men of the Corps of Discovery celebrate reaching the shore of the Pacific Ocean?

The men carved their names on trees.

Quiz-Quiz-Trade • Answer

124

United States Social Studies: Engaging Cooperative Learning Activities
Kagan Publishing • 800.933.2667 • www.KaganOnline.com

Westward Expansion
The Lewis and Clark Expedition

Directions: Cut out each card along the dotted lines. Then fold each card in half so the question is on one side and the answer is on the back. Glue or tape the cards together to keep the answers and questions on opposite sides.

17 *Westward Expansion*

Although eager to return to St. Louis, what caused the men to stay in Oregon for the winter?

Quiz-Quiz-Trade • Question

17 *Westward Expansion*

Although eager to return to St. Louis, what caused the men to stay in Oregon for the winter?

high winds and driving winds

Quiz-Quiz-Trade • Answer

18 *Westward Expansion*

Lewis and Clark returned to St. Louis on September 23, 1806, more than _____ _____ after they left.

Quiz-Quiz-Trade • Question

18 *Westward Expansion*

Lewis and Clark returned to St. Louis on September 23, 1806, more than _____ _____ after they left.

2 years

Quiz-Quiz-Trade • Answer

19 *Westward Expansion*

Quiz-Quiz-Trade • Question

19 *Westward Expansion*

Quiz-Quiz-Trade • Answer

20 *Westward Expansion*

Quiz-Quiz-Trade • Question

20 *Westward Expansion*

Quiz-Quiz-Trade • Answer

United States Social Studies: Engaging Cooperative Learning Activities
Kagan Publishing • 800.933.2667 • www.KaganOnline.com

125

Westward Expansion
The Pony Express

Name: _____

Directions: Pair up and take turns answering each question. Don't forget to get your partner's initials.

1 ★ ★ ★ ★ ★ ★ ★ ★

How much were riders offered to work for the Pony Express?

_____

_____

_____

_____

_____ Initials

2 ★ ★ ★ ★ ★ ★ ★ ★

What event brought thousands of people west to California in 1848?

_____

_____

_____

_____

_____ Initials

3 ★ ★ ★ ★ ★ ★ ★ ★

What were two causes of pioneer deaths en route to the west?

_____

_____

_____

_____

_____ Initials

4 ★ ★ ★ ★ ★ ★ ★ ★

What did a rider do if his replacement was not available?

_____

_____

_____

_____

_____ Initials

5 ★ ★ ★ ★ ★ ★ ★ ★

What are two agreements made during The Rider's Oath?

_____

_____

_____

_____

_____ Initials

6 ★ ★ ★ ★ ★ ★ ★ ★

How did Pony Express riders cross the Missouri River?

_____

_____

_____

_____

_____ Initials

7 ★ ★ ★ ★ ★ ★ ★ ★

What finally stopped the conflict between the Pony Express stations and the Paiute people?

_____

_____

_____

_____ Initials

8 ★ ★ ★ ★ ★ ★ ★ ★

What is the leather covering called that fits over the saddle and is used to carry the mail?

_____

_____

_____

_____ Initials

9 ★ ★ ★ ★ ★ ★ ★ ★

How many riders lost their life carrying mail on the Pony Express?

_____

_____

_____

_____ Initials

126

United States Social Studies: Engaging Cooperative Learning Activities
Kagan Publishing • 800.933.2667 • www.KaganOnline.com

Westward Expansion
The War of 1812

Name: _____

Directions: Pair up and take turns circling the answer to each question. Don't forget to get your partner's initials.

1

Who was president during the War of 1812?

a) George Washington
b) James Madison
c) Thomas Jefferson
d) Benjamin Franklin

_____ Initials

2

What was unique about the War of 1812 for its time?

a) The majority of war was at sea.
b) Americans fought on British land.
c) The American people voted for the war.
d) The war was funded by the sale of stocks and bonds.

_____ Initials

3

Which of the following was NOT a reason for the War of 1812?

a) France and Great Britain were attacking U.S. ships.
b) Britain was arming American Indians to attack settlers.
c) The U.S. wanted to take Canada from Great Britain.
d) The U.S. wanted to take over Great Britain's sea trade routes.

_____ Initials

4

How was American industry affected by the war?

a) Industry took a hard hit resulting in loss of jobs.
b) It prospered because more goods were made at home.
c) It increased because trades with Britain were increased.
d) A large boom occurred because France became a major supporter of the war.

_____ Initials

5

Which political party disappeared after the war due to their opposition?

a) The Democratic party
b) The Republican party
c) The Federalist party
d) The Independent party

_____ Initials

6

What nickname was given to the United States Ship, *Constitution*, after British cannons seemed to bounce off her?

a) Ironclad
b) Old Ironsides
c) Iron Women
d) Iron States

_____ Initials

7

What event happened in August 1814 when British forces came to Washington, D.C.?

a) The president was assassinated.
b) The capital city and the president's house were burned and in control of Britain.
c) Many important historical documents were seized by British forces.
d) U.S. troops surrendered to Great Britain.

_____ Initials

8

What current national symbol was created after the battle of Fort Henry?

a) The American Flag
b) The National Anthem
c) The Pledge of Allegiance
d) The Statue of Liberty

_____ Initials

9

What event led Andrew Jackson to be seen as national hero?

a) Victory at the Battle of New Orleans
b) Saving famous historic documents from the Capitol
c) Signed the treaty in Europe
d) Stopping British forces from invading from Canada

_____ Initials

United States Social Studies: Engaging Cooperative Learning Activities
Kagan Publishing • 800.933.2667 • www.KaganOnline.com

127

Westward Expansion
The Lewis and Clark Expedition

Directions: The class "mixes" until the teacher calls, "pair." Students find a new partner to discuss or answer the teacher's question.

1

Westward Expansion

Would you volunteer to join Meriwether Lewis and William Clark on their expedition to explore the Louisiana Purchase? Explain why or why not.

Mix-Pair-Share

2

Westward Expansion

Lewis and Clark recorded hundreds of new animals and plants during their journey. Which plant or animal was the most helpful to the men? Explain your thinking.

Mix-Pair-Share

3

Westward Expansion

If you were a member of the Corps of Discovery, what would have been the most difficult part of the expedition? Explain your thinking.

Mix-Pair-Share

4

Westward Expansion

If you were able to go back in time to join the Corps of Discovery, what is one modern piece of technology would you take with you and why? Explain.

Mix-Pair-Share

5

Westward Expansion

Imagine you are ready to join the Corps of Discovery. You are packing your small bag for the expedition. What would you put into it? Why? Please explain.

Mix-Pair-Share

6

Westward Expansion

Your teacher has asked you to write a report from the viewpoint of someone in the Corps of Discovery. Who would you choose and why?

Mix-Pair-Share

7

Westward Expansion

Imagine you had the opportunity to interview Meriwether Lewis or William Clark. What would be three questions you would ask him and why?

Mix-Pair-Share

8

Westward Expansion

You have been asked by the United States government to write a simple poem about Lewis and Clark to put at the bottom of their statue. What are three lines in your poem?

Mix-Pair-Share

9

Westward Expansion

How would have the Lewis and Clark Expedition been different had Sacagawea not joined the journey? Explain your thinking.

Mix-Pair-Share

10

Westward Expansion

If you wanted to learn more about the Lewis and Clark Expedition, what are three questions you would like to research? Where would you look for your information?

Mix-Pair-Share

United States Social Studies: Engaging Cooperative Learning Activities
Kagan Publishing • 800.933.2667 • www.KaganOnline.com

Westward Expansion
The Pony Express

Directions: The class "mixes" until the teacher calls, "pair." Students find a new partner to discuss or answer the teacher's question.

① Westward Expansion

Would you have liked to work as a Pony Express rider? Why or why not?

Mix-Pair-Share

② Westward Expansion

In your opinion, why were most Pony Express riders young men?

Mix-Pair-Share

③ Westward Expansion

What do you believe was the hardest challenge for the Pony Express riders?

Mix-Pair-Share

④ Westward Expansion

Was the Pony Express successful? Explain your thinking?

Mix-Pair-Share

⑤ Westward Expansion

What changes would you make if you were working for the Pony Express?

Mix-Pair-Share

⑥ Westward Expansion

Why do you think there were no women working as Pony Express riders?

Mix-Pair-Share

⑦ Westward Expansion

What important role did the Home Stations provide to the Pony Express?

Mix-Pair-Share

⑧ Westward Expansion

Were the Pony Express riders treated fairly while working? Explain your thinking.

Mix-Pair-Share

United States Social Studies: Engaging Cooperative Learning Activities
Kagan Publishing • 800.933.2667 • www.KaganOnline.com

129

Westward Expansion
The Pony Express

Directions: The class "mixes" until the teacher calls, "pair." Students find a new partner to discuss or answer the teacher's question.

---

9 Westward Expansion

What important roles did women play in the Pony Express? Explain your thinking.

Mix-Pair-Share

---

10 Westward Expansion

Was it fair to expect Pony Express riders to keep riding if there was no replacement? What about the horses? Explain your thinking.

Mix-Pair-Share

---

11 Westward Expansion

What other jobs were available in the Pony Express besides being a rider? What job would you like to work? Explain.

Mix-Pair-Share

---

12 Westward Expansion

In your opinion, what was the most important event that occurred during the time of the Pony Express? Explain your thinking.

Mix-Pair-Share

---

13 Westward Expansion

How did the Pony Express play an important role in the election of President Abraham Lincoln and the Civil War? Explain.

Mix-Pair-Share

---

14 Westward Expansion

In your opinion, was the Pony Express safe for the riders? Justify your thinking.

Mix-Pair-Share

---

15 Westward Expansion

What do you believe to be the most important piece of equipment to the Pony Express rider? Explain your thinking.

Mix-Pair-Share

---

16 Westward Expansion

What is ONE piece of modern, handheld technology that would most benefit the Pony Express rider? Explain your thinking.

Mix-Pair-Share

United States Social Studies: Engaging Cooperative Learning Activities
Kagan Publishing • 800.933.2667 • www.KaganOnline.com

The Civil War and Reconstruction

Cooperative Learning Activities

The Civil War and Reconstruction
The Struggles of War

Directions: Think about the prompt, and then write your own response. When done, RoundRobin share your writing with your teammates. Use the space at the bottom to record ideas your teammates share.

Prompt: Which side, Union or Confederacy, had the greatest difficulty during the war? Use examples from history in your answer.

My writing: _____

_____

_____

_____

_____

_____

_____

_____

_____

_____

Ideas Teammates Share

United States Social Studies: Engaging Cooperative Learning Activities
Kagan Publishing • 800.933.2667 • www.KaganOnline.com

The Civil War and Reconstruction

The Most Important Event of the Civil War

Directions: Think about the prompt, and then write your own response. When done, RoundRobin share your writing with your teammates. Use the space at the bottom to record ideas your teammates share.

Prompt: Which was the most important event during the Civil War? Use history details to support your answer.

My writing: _____

_____

_____

_____

_____

_____

_____

_____

_____

_____

Ideas Teammates Share

United States Social Studies: Engaging Cooperative Learning Activities
Kagan Publishing • 800.933.2667 • www.KaganOnline.com

133

The Civil War and Reconstruction

A Soldier's Letter Home

Directions: Think about the prompt, and then write your own response. When done, RoundRobin share your writing with your teammates. Use the space at the bottom to record ideas your teammates share.

Prompt: Imagine you are a Union or Confederate soldier and write a letter home describing life in camp, on the battlefields, and the war.

My writing: _____

_____

_____

_____

_____

_____

_____

_____

_____

_____

_____

Ideas Teammates Share

United States Social Studies: Engaging Cooperative Learning Activities
Kagan Publishing • 800.933.2667 • www.KaganOnline.com

The Civil War and Reconstruction
The Greatest Cause of the Civil War

Directions: Think about the prompt, and then write your own response. When done, RoundRobin share your writing with your teammates. Use the space at the bottom to record ideas your teammates share.

Prompt: In your opinion, what was the greatest cause of the Civil War? Describe using details from history.

My writing: _____

_____

_____

_____

_____

_____

_____

_____

_____

_____

Ideas Teammates Share

United States Social Studies: **Engaging Cooperative Learning Activities**
Kagan Publishing • 800.933.2667 • www.KaganOnline.com

135

The Civil War and Reconstruction
A Slave's Life

Directions: Think about the prompt, and then write your own response. When done, RoundRobin share your writing with your teammates. Use the space at the bottom to record ideas your teammates share.

Prompt: Issues over slavery were one cause of the Civil War. Describe events of a slave's life before the Civil War.

My writing: _____

_____

_____

_____

_____

_____

_____

_____

_____

_____

_____

Ideas Teammates Share

136

United States Social Studies: Engaging Cooperative Learning Activities
Kagan Publishing • 800.933.2667 • www.KaganOnline.com

The Civil War and Reconstruction
Northern and Southern States

■ **RallyCoach Directions:** Take turns answering each question as your partner coaches. Explain your thinking to your coach.
■ **Sage-N-Scribe Directions:** The Sage describes what he or she knows about the question so the Scribe can answer the question. The Sage and Scribe switch roles for each question.

Name _____

1. Which sentence best describes the difference between the northern states and southern states regarding geography?
   a) People in the north lived in cities spread out among the state whereas people in the south lived close together.
   b) People in the south often walked to industry jobs while people in the north worked on their own land.
   c) People in the north worked in factories located in cities when people in the south lived a rural way of life working on farms.
   d) There were no geographical differences between northern states and southern states.

2. The northern states and southern states had different opinions regarding tariffs. What is a tariff?
   a) Tax on imported goods
   b) Ability to own slaves
   c) Tax on working men
   d) Special factories in the north

3. Which of the following states were considered border states, states that continued to own slaves but did not secede from the north?
   a) Missouri
   b) Texas
   c) Tennessee
   d) Connecticut

Name _____

1. Which of the following was NOT a cause of the Civil War?
   a) The practice of using slavery in the south
   b) The southern states arguing to secede from the northern states
   c) The Continental Congress publicly announcing the end of owning slaves
   d) The northern economy practicing free labor verses the southern economy using slave labor

2. What was the belief of abolitionists?
   a) Only property-owning white men should be allowed to vote.
   b) Slavery is wrong and should be ended.
   c) Tariffs should be imposed on those importing goods.
   d) The south should secede from the north.

3. Which of the following events occurred first?
   a) German William T. Sherman's Union Army sets fire to Atlanta, Georgia.
   b) Abraham Lincoln is elected president.
   c) The Battle of Bull Run
   d) Confederate General Robert E. Lee surrenders to Union General Ulysses S. Grant.

United States Social Studies: Engaging Cooperative Learning Activities
Kagan Publishing • 800.933.2667 • www.KaganOnline.com

137

The Civil War and Reconstruction
Ulysses S. Grant

■ **RallyCoach Directions:** Take turns answering each question as your partner coaches. Explain your thinking to your coach.
■ **Sage-N-Scribe Directions:** The Sage describes what he or she knows about the question so the Scribe can answer the question. The Sage and Scribe switch roles for each question.

Name _____

1. **Which of the following is true about both Ulysses S. Grant and Robert E. Lee?**
   a) Both men were born in Virginia.
   b) Both men were the oldest son's within their families.
   c) Both men attended the U.S. Military Academy at West Point.
   d) Both men struggled through academics.

2. **Aside from serving in the military, what other position did Ulysses S. Grant serve the country?**
   a) He was the first Veterans Hospital Administrator.
   b) He was vice president to Abraham Lincoln.
   c) He was the 18th president.
   d) He was War Advisor to the Air Force.

3. **Which event, in 1862, is often credited as the earliest significant Union victory?**
   a) The assault on Fort Donelson
   b) The First Battle of Bull Run
   c) The Battle of Shiloh
   d) The Missouri Compromise

4. **Which of the following sentences best describes Ulysses S. Grant's childhood?**
   a) He grew up a son of a wealthy southern man.
   b) He was born in Ohio as the son of a wealthy leather tanner.
   c) He apprenticed in his father's business in hopes of taking it over as an adult.
   d) He was an only child of his widowed mother.

Name _____

1. **What role did Ulysses S. Grant serve during the Civil War?**
   a) He was the President of the United States in 1860.
   b) He was the Leader of the Confederate Army.
   c) He was the Commander of the Union Army.
   d) He was the Writer of *Uncle Tom's Cabin*.

2. **What war did Ulysses S. Grant leave to go fight in 1846?**
   a) The Spanish-American War
   b) The Civil War
   c) The French and Indian War
   d) The Revolutionary War

3. **What profession did Ulysses S. Grant pursue after resigning his commission?**
   a) Farming
   b) Banker
   c) Horse training
   d) Military instructor

4. **Which of the following sentences best describe Grant's skills with horses?**
   a) His understanding of horses lead to a job of training horses.
   b) He was afraid of horses after a childhood fall but later learned to ride as a general.
   c) He was fascinated by other boys' racing horses but could not own his own horse.
   d) His skill came from extensive training from his father.

138

United States Social Studies: Engaging Cooperative Learning Activities
Kagan Publishing • 800.933.2667 • www.KaganOnline.com

The Civil War and Reconstruction
Reconstruction

■ **RallyCoach Directions:** Take turns answering each question as your partner coaches. Explain your thinking to your coach.
■ **Sage-N-Scribe Directions:** The Sage describes what he or she knows about the question so the Scribe can answer the question. The Sage and Scribe switch roles for each question.

Name _____

1. **What event happened less than a week after the surrender of the Confederate armies to the Union?**
   a) General Lee was taken into custody and tried for war crimes committed against the union.
   b) The southern farmers protested the surrender and what would be their way of life by burning down their own crops.
   c) President Lincoln was assassinated while attending a production at Ford's Theatre.
   d) The Emancipation Proclamation was given and granted slaves their freedom.

2. **As a reaction to the end of slavery, the southern states passed laws called Black Codes. What are Black Codes?**
   a) Laws that limit the rights of freed former slaves.
   b) Laws that allow former slaves the right to vote if they own land.
   c) Laws that do not allow former slaves to work outside of former slave positions.
   d) Laws that grant former slaves the same rights as white Americans.

3. **Which of the following is NOT an effect of the Reconstruction?**
   a) Carpetbaggers moved to the south from the north and often started new businesses.
   b) Scalawags, southern supporters of reconstruction, were accused of the hardships in the south.
   c) A group of white southern men developed the Ku Klux Klan to restore control over former slaves.
   d) Andrew Johnson was removed from office following his impeachment.

Name _____

1. **What did the Thirteenth Amendment accomplish?**
   a) Allowed former slaves to take over the plantations of former owners
   b) Abolished slavery in all states
   c) Readmitted the former Confederate states back into the Union
   d) Provided provisions for newly freed slaves in the form of jobs, money, and work with their former slave owners

2. **What was established to help former slaves adjust to free life by building schools, hospitals, and more?**
   a) Jim Crow Laws
   b) Reconstruction Act
   c) Freedmen's Bureau
   d) Ku Klux Klan

3. **What are Jim Crow laws?**
   a) A law stating a person could only vote if his grandfather voted before 1867
   b) A law that enforced the segregation between white Americans and former slaves
   c) A law allowing sharecropping to be used as a way for freed African Americans to earn a living
   d) A law preventing any man from voting if he could not pass a reading test

United States Social Studies: Engaging Cooperative Learning Activities
Kagan Publishing • 800.933.2667 • www.KaganOnline.com

139

The Civil War and Reconstruction
Facts and Outcomes

Directions: Cut out each card along the dotted lines. Then fold each card in half so the question is on one side and the answer is on the back. Glue or tape the cards together to keep the answers and questions on opposite sides.

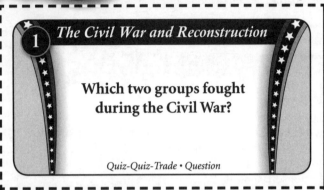

1 *The Civil War and Reconstruction*

Which two groups fought during the Civil War?

Quiz-Quiz-Trade • Question

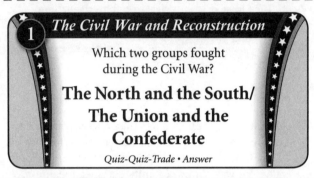

1 *The Civil War and Reconstruction*

Which two groups fought during the Civil War?

The North and the South/ The Union and the Confederate

Quiz-Quiz-Trade • Answer

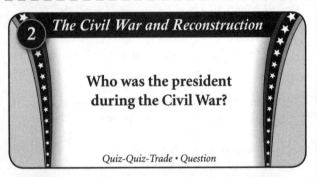

2 *The Civil War and Reconstruction*

Who was the president during the Civil War?

Quiz-Quiz-Trade • Question

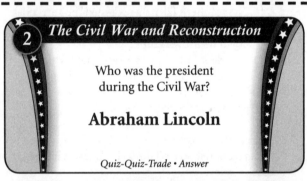

2 *The Civil War and Reconstruction*

Who was the president during the Civil War?

Abraham Lincoln

Quiz-Quiz-Trade • Answer

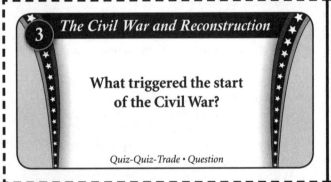

3 *The Civil War and Reconstruction*

What triggered the start of the Civil War?

Quiz-Quiz-Trade • Question

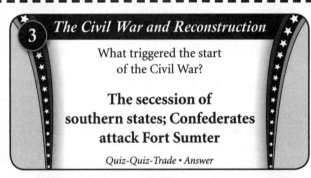

3 *The Civil War and Reconstruction*

What triggered the start of the Civil War?

The secession of southern states; Confederates attack Fort Sumter

Quiz-Quiz-Trade • Answer

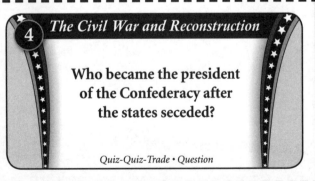

4 *The Civil War and Reconstruction*

Who became the president of the Confederacy after the states seceded?

Quiz-Quiz-Trade • Question

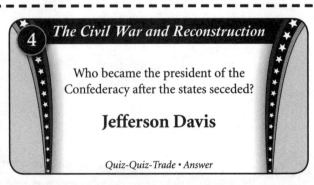

4 *The Civil War and Reconstruction*

Who became the president of the Confederacy after the states seceded?

Jefferson Davis

Quiz-Quiz-Trade • Answer

140

United States Social Studies: Engaging Cooperative Learning Activities
Kagan Publishing • 800.933.2667 • www.KaganOnline.com

The Civil War and Reconstruction
Facts and Outcomes

Directions: Cut out each card along the dotted lines. Then fold each card in half so the question is on one side and the answer is on the back. Glue or tape the cards together to keep the answers and questions on opposite sides.

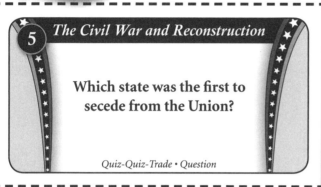

5 The Civil War and Reconstruction

Which state was the first to secede from the Union?

Quiz-Quiz-Trade • Question

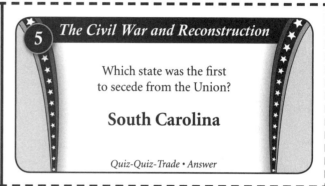

5 The Civil War and Reconstruction

Which state was the first to secede from the Union?

South Carolina

Quiz-Quiz-Trade • Answer

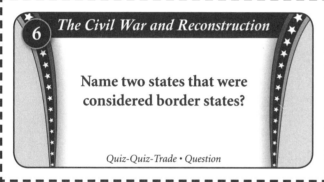

6 The Civil War and Reconstruction

Name two states that were considered border states?

Quiz-Quiz-Trade • Question

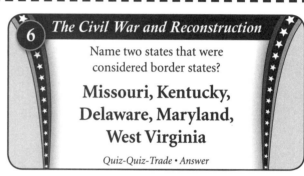

6 The Civil War and Reconstruction

Name two states that were considered border states?

Missouri, Kentucky, Delaware, Maryland, West Virginia

Quiz-Quiz-Trade • Answer

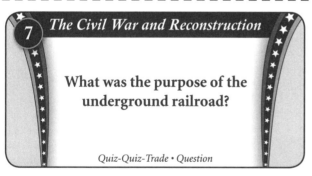

7 The Civil War and Reconstruction

What was the purpose of the underground railroad?

Quiz-Quiz-Trade • Question

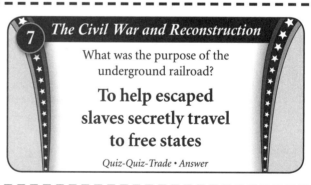

7 The Civil War and Reconstruction

What was the purpose of the underground railroad?

To help escaped slaves secretly travel to free states

Quiz-Quiz-Trade • Answer

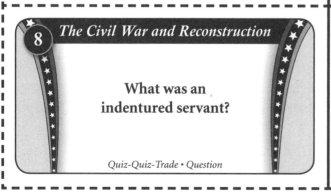

8 The Civil War and Reconstruction

What was an indentured servant?

Quiz-Quiz-Trade • Question

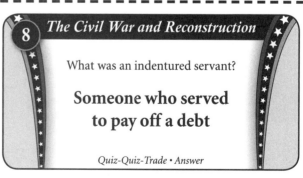

8 The Civil War and Reconstruction

What was an indentured servant?

Someone who served to pay off a debt

Quiz-Quiz-Trade • Answer

United States Social Studies: Engaging Cooperative Learning Activities
Kagan Publishing • 800.933.2667 • www.KaganOnline.com

141

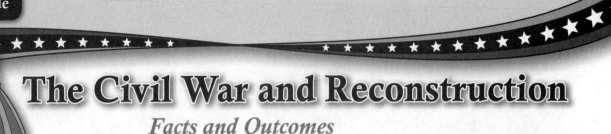

The Civil War and Reconstruction
Facts and Outcomes

Directions: Cut out each card along the dotted lines. Then fold each card in half so the question is on one side and the answer is on the back. Glue or tape the cards together to keep the answers and questions on opposite sides.

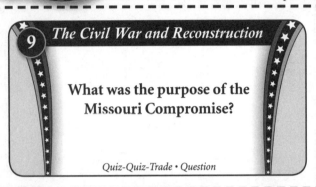

9 — *The Civil War and Reconstruction*

What was the purpose of the Missouri Compromise?

Quiz-Quiz-Trade • Question

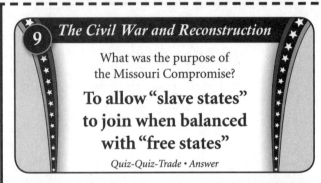

9 — *The Civil War and Reconstruction*

What was the purpose of the Missouri Compromise?

To allow "slave states" to join when balanced with "free states"

Quiz-Quiz-Trade • Answer

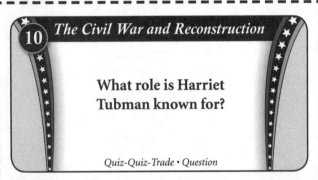

10 — *The Civil War and Reconstruction*

What role is Harriet Tubman known for?

Quiz-Quiz-Trade • Question

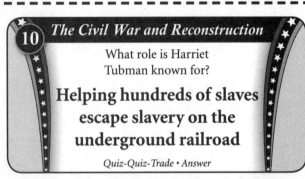

10 — *The Civil War and Reconstruction*

What role is Harriet Tubman known for?

Helping hundreds of slaves escape slavery on the underground railroad

Quiz-Quiz-Trade • Answer

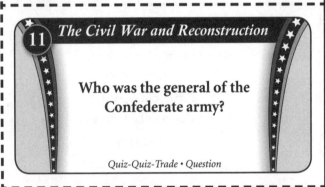

11 — *The Civil War and Reconstruction*

Who was the general of the Confederate army?

Quiz-Quiz-Trade • Question

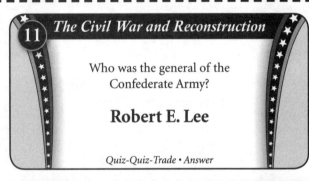

11 — *The Civil War and Reconstruction*

Who was the general of the Confederate Army?

Robert E. Lee

Quiz-Quiz-Trade • Answer

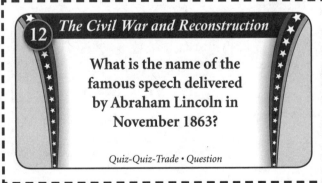

12 — *The Civil War and Reconstruction*

What is the name of the famous speech delivered by Abraham Lincoln in November 1863?

Quiz-Quiz-Trade • Question

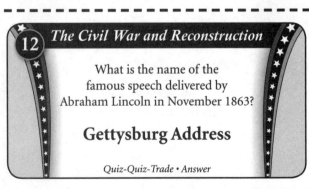

12 — *The Civil War and Reconstruction*

What is the name of the famous speech delivered by Abraham Lincoln in November 1863?

Gettysburg Address

Quiz-Quiz-Trade • Answer

United States Social Studies: Engaging Cooperative Learning Activities
Kagan Publishing • 800.933.2667 • www.KaganOnline.com

The Civil War and Reconstruction
Facts and Outcomes

Directions: Cut out each card along the dotted lines. Then fold each card in half so the question is on one side and the answer is on the back. Glue or tape the cards together to keep the answers and questions on opposite sides.

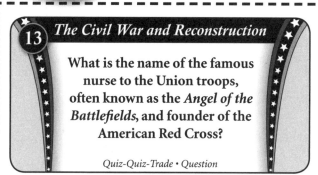

13 *The Civil War and Reconstruction*

What is the name of the famous nurse to the Union troops, often known as the *Angel of the Battlefields*, and founder of the American Red Cross?

Quiz-Quiz-Trade • Question

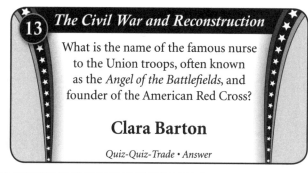

13 *The Civil War and Reconstruction*

What is the name of the famous nurse to the Union troops, often known as the *Angel of the Battlefields*, and founder of the American Red Cross?

Clara Barton

Quiz-Quiz-Trade • Answer

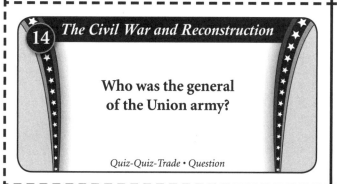

14 *The Civil War and Reconstruction*

Who was the general of the Union army?

Quiz-Quiz-Trade • Question

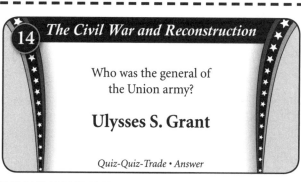

14 *The Civil War and Reconstruction*

Who was the general of the Union army?

Ulysses S. Grant

Quiz-Quiz-Trade • Answer

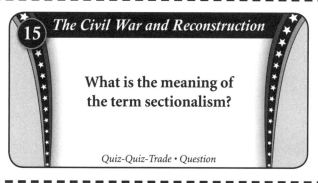

15 *The Civil War and Reconstruction*

What is the meaning of the term sectionalism?

Quiz-Quiz-Trade • Question

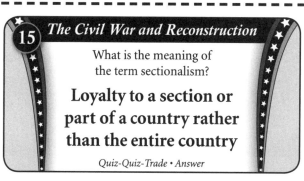

15 *The Civil War and Reconstruction*

What is the meaning of the term sectionalism?

Loyalty to a section or part of a country rather than the entire country

Quiz-Quiz-Trade • Answer

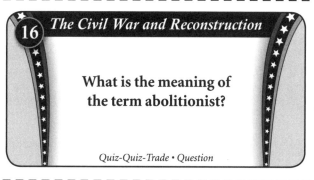

16 *The Civil War and Reconstruction*

What is the meaning of the term abolitionist?

Quiz-Quiz-Trade • Question

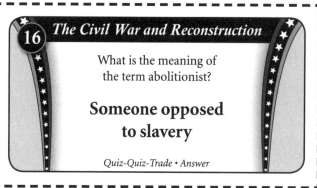

16 *The Civil War and Reconstruction*

What is the meaning of the term abolitionist?

Someone opposed to slavery

Quiz-Quiz-Trade • Answer

United States Social Studies: Engaging Cooperative Learning Activities
Kagan Publishing • 800.933.2667 • www.KaganOnline.com

143

The Civil War and Reconstruction
Facts and Outcomes

Directions: Cut out each card along the dotted lines. Then fold each card in half so the question is on one side and the answer is on the back. Glue or tape the cards together to keep the answers and questions on opposite sides.

---

17 *The Civil War and Reconstruction*

What was the difference of opinion between the northern states and the southern states regarding tariffs?

Quiz-Quiz-Trade • Question

---

17 *The Civil War and Reconstruction*

What was the difference of opinion between the northern states and the southern states regarding tariffs?

The northern states wanted higher tariffs; the southern states lower tariffs

Quiz-Quiz-Trade • Answer

---

18 *The Civil War and Reconstruction*

What was difference between the northern states and the southern states regarding industry?

Quiz-Quiz-Trade • Question

---

18 *The Civil War and Reconstruction*

What was difference between the northern states and the southern states regarding industry?

Northern states had factories, southern states grew crops

Quiz-Quiz-Trade • Answer

---

19 *The Civil War and Reconstruction*

Quiz-Quiz-Trade • Question

---

19 *The Civil War and Reconstruction*

Quiz-Quiz-Trade • Answer

---

20 *The Civil War and Reconstruction*

Quiz-Quiz-Trade • Question

---

20 *The Civil War and Reconstruction*

Quiz-Quiz-Trade • Answer

144

United States Social Studies: Engaging Cooperative Learning Activities
Kagan Publishing • 800.933.2667 • www.KaganOnline.com

The Civil War and Reconstruction
Union and Confederacy

Name: _____

Directions: Pair up and take turns answering each question. Don't forget to get your partner's initials.

1 What was one advantage the Confederacy had during the Civil War?

_____
_____
_____
_____

_____ Initials

2 What was one advantage the Union had during the Civil War?

_____
_____
_____
_____

_____ Initials

3 Why did Britain not send soldiers in support of the Confederacy when they imported cotton from the south?

_____
_____
_____

_____ Initials

4 The Union used a blockade of the Atlantic and Gulf coasts as part of the Anaconda Plan. What is a blockade?

_____
_____
_____

_____ Initials

5 Where was the location of the Confederacy's capitol?

_____
_____
_____

_____ Initials

6 What battle on September 17, 1862, was an important victory for the Union as it ended any southern support from Britain?

_____
_____
_____

_____ Initials

7 Slave codes were a large part of the slave's life. What is a Black Code?

_____
_____
_____
_____

_____ Initials

8 What event happened on September 2, 1864, and was a big win for the Union?

_____
_____
_____

_____ Initials

9 Both the Confederate and the Union passed draft laws. What is a draft?

_____
_____
_____
_____

_____ Initials

United States Social Studies: Engaging Cooperative Learning Activities
Kagan Publishing • 800.933.2667 • www.KaganOnline.com

145

The Civil War and Reconstruction
Robert E. Lee

Name: _____

Directions: Pair up and take turns circling the answer to each question. Don't forget to get your partner's initials.

1

In which state was Robert E. Lee born?

a) Missouri
b) New York
c) Alabama
d) Virginia

Initials _____

2

Which sentence best describes Robert E. Lee's upbringing?

a) His father died when he was 11, and his mother instilled strong moral values.
b) His father was a tough man demanding high expectations of his only son.
c) He was raised solely by his father after his mother died during childbirth.
d) He did poorly in school and this reflected badly on his prominent father.

Initials _____

3

What caused Robert E. Lee to consider attending the U.S. Military Academy at West Point?

a) His father talked to the Dean of Admissions.
b) The academy was free to men from Virginia, and he was the son of a war hero.
c) His mother personally talked to the academy.
d) His older brothers had attended and graduated with honors.

Initials _____

4

Which of the following is evidence of Robert E. Lee's hardworking nature?

a) He never lost a battle during war.
b) He graduated second in his class from West Point without any demerits.
c) He diligently wrote letters to his mother and father at wartime.
d) He married Mary Custis, granddaughter of Martha Washington.

Initials _____

5

Why did Robert E. Lee refuse President Lincoln's offer to lead the Union Army?

a) He believed in the practice of owning slaves.
b) He did not feel he could lead a large army.
c) Virginia seceded and he did not want to fight against his home and family.
d) He felt the war was unjust and un-American.

Initials _____

6

What feelings did Robert E. Lee have towards slavery?

a) He felt it was necessary to allow the southern states to compete with northern state commerce.
b) He considered slavery a moral and political evil and rejoiced in the abolishment of slavery.
c) He owned many slaves and felt it the right of Confederate soldiers.
d) His wife, a northerner, refused to own slaves.

Initials _____

7

What career did Lee pursue following his military career?

a) President of Washington College
b) Newspaper reporter
c) Military instructor
d) He retired

Initials _____

8

Which event occurred at Lee's burial?

a) He was buried next to his wife.
b) Traveler, his horse, walked behind Lee's casket.
c) He was honored for his service to the Union.
d) His children did not attend.

Initials _____

9

Why was Lee not granted U.S. citizenship immediately following the war?

a) He refused to take the oath.
b) His papers were never processed.
c) As general of Confederacy, he was not allowed.
d) He did not feel worthy.

Initials _____

United States Social Studies: Engaging Cooperative Learning Activities
Kagan Publishing • 800.933.2667 • www.KaganOnline.com

The Civil War and Reconstruction
People of the Civil War

Directions: Cut out cards along the dotted lines. Distribute one card per student in sequence so for every student with a people card, there is a student with a matching description card. Students use cards to play Mix-N-Match.

The Civil War and Reconstruction

What is the following person known for regarding the Civil War?

Clara Barton

Mix-N-Match

The Civil War and Reconstruction

Who is known for this action during the Civil War?
Founded the Red Cross in 1881 after nursing wounded soldiers during the Civil War

Mix-N-Match

The Civil War and Reconstruction

What is the following person known for regarding the Civil War?

Robert Shaw

Mix-N-Match

The Civil War and Reconstruction

Who is known for this action during the Civil War?
Commander of the 54th Regiment, which was one of the first African American units serving in the Civil War

Mix-N-Match

The Civil War and Reconstruction

What is the following person known for regarding the Civil War?

Robert E. Lee

Mix-N-Match

The Civil War and Reconstruction

Who is known for this action during the Civil War?
General of the Confederate Army

Mix-N-Match

The Civil War and Reconstruction

What is the following person known for regarding the Civil War?

Ulysses S. Grant

Mix-N-Match

The Civil War and Reconstruction

Who is known for this action during the Civil War?
Fourth general to lead the Union forces, later elected president for two terms

Mix-N-Match

United States Social Studies: Engaging Cooperative Learning Activities
Kagan Publishing • 800.933.2667 • www.KaganOnline.com

147

The Civil War and Reconstruction
People of the Civil War

Directions: Cut out cards along the dotted lines. Distribute one card per student in sequence so for every student with a people card, there is a student with a matching description card. Students use cards to play Mix-N-Match.

The Civil War and Reconstruction What is the following person known for regarding the Civil War? **Harriet Tubman**	*The Civil War and Reconstruction* Who is known for this action during the Civil War? **Famous "conductor" of the underground railroad after escaping slavery herself**
The Civil War and Reconstruction What is the following person known for regarding the Civil War? **Harriet Beecher Stowe**	*The Civil War and Reconstruction* Who is known for this action during the Civil War? **Author of *Uncle Tom's Cabin* depicting the cruelty of slavery**
The Civil War and Reconstruction What is the following person known for regarding the Civil War? **Abraham Lincoln**	*The Civil War and Reconstruction* Who is known for this action during the Civil War? **Republican elected the 16th President of the United States in 1860**
The Civil War and Reconstruction What is the following person known for regarding the Civil War? **Stephen Douglas**	*The Civil War and Reconstruction* Who is known for this action during the Civil War? **Democratic senator who ran against Lincoln for president**

United States Social Studies: Engaging Cooperative Learning Activities
Kagan Publishing • 800.933.2667 • www.KaganOnline.com

The Civil War and Reconstruction
People of the Civil War

Directions: Cut out cards along the dotted lines. Distribute one card per student in sequence so for every student with a people card, there is a student with a matching description card. Students use cards to play Mix-N-Match.

The Civil War and Reconstruction

What is the following person known for regarding the Civil War?

Jefferson Davis

Mix-N-Match

The Civil War and Reconstruction

Who is known for this action during the Civil War?
Senator from Mississippi elected President of the Confederacy

Mix-N-Match

The Civil War and Reconstruction

What is the following person known for regarding the Civil War?

Thomas "Stonewall" Jackson

Mix-N-Match

The Civil War and Reconstruction

Who is known for this action during the Civil War?
General from Virginia who defeated the Union army in Virginia, fought in the first Battle of Bull Run

Mix-N-Match

The Civil War and Reconstruction

What is the following person known for regarding the Civil War?

General Winfield Scott

Mix-N-Match

The Civil War and Reconstruction

Who is known for this action during the Civil War?
Fought in the Mexican-American War and provided advice on war strategy to President Lincoln

Mix-N-Match

The Civil War and Reconstruction

What is the following person known for regarding the Civil War?

Henry Clay

Mix-N-Match

The Civil War and Reconstruction

Who is known for this action during the Civil War?
Known as "The Great Compromise" and proposed the Missouri Compromise

Mix-N-Match

United States Social Studies: Engaging Cooperative Learning Activities
Kagan Publishing • 800.933.2667 • www.KaganOnline.com

149

The Civil War and Reconstruction

Key People, Terms, and Events

Directions: Copy cards, one per student. Cut out each card along the dotted lines and follow the directions for Who Am I?

1

The Civil War and Reconstruction

Sectionalism

Who Am I?

2

The Civil War and Reconstruction

Harriet Tubman

Who Am I?

3

The Civil War and Reconstruction

Underground Railroad

Who Am I?

4

The Civil War and Reconstruction

Missouri Compromise

Who Am I?

150

United States Social Studies: Engaging Cooperative Learning Activities
Kagan Publishing • 800.933.2667 • www.KaganOnline.com

The Civil War and Reconstruction

Key People, Terms, and Events

Directions: Copy cards, one per student. Cut out each card along the dotted lines and follow the directions for Who Am I?

5

The Civil War and Reconstruction

Harriet Beecher Stowe

Who Am I?

6

The Civil War and Reconstruction

Abraham Lincoln

Who Am I?

7

The Civil War and Reconstruction

Fugitive Slave Laws

Who Am I?

8

The Civil War and Reconstruction

Confederacy

Who Am I?

United States Social Studies: Engaging Cooperative Learning Activities
Kagan Publishing • 800.933.2667 • www.KaganOnline.com

151

The Civil War and Reconstruction

Key People, Terms, and Events

Directions: Copy cards, one per student. Cut out each card along the dotted lines and follow the directions for Who Am I?

9

The Civil War and Reconstruction

Union

Who Am I?

10

The Civil War and Reconstruction

Jefferson Davis

Who Am I?

11

The Civil War and Reconstruction

Border States

Who Am I?

12

The Civil War and Reconstruction

Robert E. Lee

Who Am I?

United States Social Studies: Engaging Cooperative Learning Activities
Kagan Publishing • 800.933.2667 • www.KaganOnline.com

The Civil War and Reconstruction

Key People, Terms, and Events

Directions: Copy cards, one per student. Cut out each card along the dotted lines and follow the directions for Who Am I?

13

The Civil War and Reconstruction

Ulysses S. Grant

Who Am I?

14

The Civil War and Reconstruction

Emancipation Proclamation

Who Am I?

15

The Civil War and Reconstruction

Fort Wagner

Who Am I?

16

The Civil War and Reconstruction

Clara Barton

Who Am I?

United States Social Studies: Engaging Cooperative Learning Activities
Kagan Publishing • 800.933.2667 • www.KaganOnline.com

153

The Civil War and Reconstruction
Key People, Terms, and Events

Directions: Copy cards, one per student. Cut out each card along the dotted lines and follow the directions for Who Am I?

(17)

The Civil War and Reconstruction

Battle of Gettysburg

Who Am I?

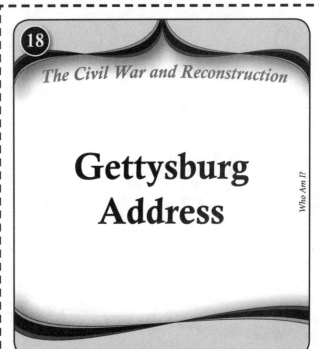

(18)

The Civil War and Reconstruction

Gettysburg Address

Who Am I?

(19)

The Civil War and Reconstruction

Thirteenth Amendment

Who Am I?

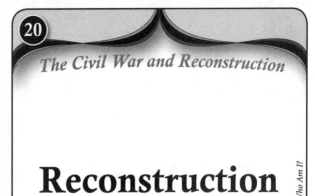

(20)

The Civil War and Reconstruction

Reconstruction

Who Am I?

154

United States Social Studies: Engaging Cooperative Learning Activities
Kagan Publishing • 800.933.2667 • www.KaganOnline.com

The Civil War and Reconstruction

Key People, Terms, and Events

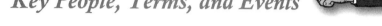

Directions: Copy cards, one per student. Cut out each card along the dotted lines and follow the directions for Who Am I?

21

The Civil War and Reconstruction

Abolitionists

Who Am I?

22

The Civil War and Reconstruction

Fredrick Douglas

Who Am I?

23

The Civil War and Reconstruction

Who Am I?

24

The Civil War and Reconstruction

Who Am I?

United States Social Studies: Engaging Cooperative Learning Activities
Kagan Publishing • 800.933.2667 • www.KaganOnline.com

155

The Civil War and Reconstruction
Conditions and Strategies

Directions: The class "mixes" until the teacher calls, "pair." Students find a new partner to discuss or answer the teacher's question.

1 *The Civil War and Reconstruction*

Describe the Emancipation Proclamation. What impact did it have on the Civil War?

Mix-Pair-Share

2 *The Civil War and Reconstruction*

Describe the life of a soldier in the Civil War. In your opinion, was it harder for a Union soldier or a Confederate Soldier? Explain your reasoning.

Mix-Pair-Share

3 *The Civil War and Reconstruction*

What roles did African Americans play during the war? How did their role change throughout the Civil War?

Mix-Pair-Share

4 *The Civil War and Reconstruction*

What roles did women play during the Civil War? Describe those using details from history.

Mix-Pair-Share

5 *The Civil War and Reconstruction*

In your opinion, what battle was the most significant in the Union's win over the Confederate? Explain your reasoning.

Mix-Pair-Share

6 *The Civil War and Reconstruction*

What impact did President Abraham Lincoln's *Gettysburg Address* have on the country? Justify your thinking.

Mix-Pair-Share

7 *The Civil War and Reconstruction*

The use of photographs helped families far away from battle get a glimpse of a soldier's life. Do you think this helped or harmed the viewpoints on the war? Explain.

Mix-Pair-Share

8 *The Civil War and Reconstruction*

General Sherman used the idea of total war as his military strategy and the basis of "Sherman's March." Describe this strategy. Do you think it is an effective strategy in war? Explain.

Mix-Pair-Share

United States Social Studies: Engaging Cooperative Learning Activities
Kagan Publishing • 800.933.2667 • www.KaganOnline.com

156

The Civil War and Reconstruction
Conditions and Strategies

Directions: The class "mixes" until the teacher calls, "pair." Students find a new partner to discuss or answer the teacher's question.

---

9 *The Civil War and Reconstruction*

How did the differences in the north and south lead to the Civil War? Explain.

In your opinion, what is the greatest difference?

Mix-Pair-Share

---

10 *The Civil War and Reconstruction*

Describe some ways slaves resisted slavery. Did these actions help or harm their cause?

Mix-Pair-Share

---

11 *The Civil War and Reconstruction*

What role did the railroad play in the Civil War? How would the war be different had the railroad not yet existed?

Mix-Pair-Share

---

12 *The Civil War and Reconstruction*

Describe the life of a slave before the Civil War. Use details in history to support your answer.

Mix-Pair-Share

---

13 *The Civil War and Reconstruction*

Describe the impact of the underground railroad. How would life for slaves been different without the underground railroad? Explain.

Mix-Pair-Share

---

14 *The Civil War and Reconstruction*

What personality traits made Ulysses S. Grant a great leader for the Union? Explain your thinking.

Mix-Pair-Share

---

15 *The Civil War and Reconstruction*

Robert E. Lee is quoted as saying, *"I have not been able to make up my mind to raise my hand against my relatives, my children, my home,"* regarding his opportunity to lead the Union. How did this affect his decision to fight with the Confederacy?

Mix-Pair-Share

---

16 *The Civil War and Reconstruction*

Generals Lee and Grant met to discuss surrender of the Confederate to the Union armies. Describe the conditions of the surrender. In your opinion, were these conditions fair or unfair? Describe your thinking.

Mix-Pair-Share

United States Social Studies: Engaging Cooperative Learning Activities
Kagan Publishing • 800.933.2667 • www.KaganOnline.com

157

Cooperative Learning Activities

Industrialization
The Spanish-American War

Directions: Think about the prompt, and then write your own response. When done, RoundRobin share your writing with your teammates. Use the space at the bottom to record ideas your teammates share.

Prompt: Describe the role newspapers played in prompting the Spanish-American war. How might this be different in today's society?

My writing: _____

_____

_____

_____

_____

_____

_____

_____

_____

_____

Ideas Teammates Share

160

United States Social Studies: Engaging Cooperative Learning Activities
Kagan Publishing • 800.933.2667 • www.KaganOnline.com

Industrialization
The Rise of Labor Laws

Directions: Think about the prompt, and then write your own response. When done, RoundRobin share your writing with your teammates. Use the space at the bottom to record ideas your teammates share.

Prompt: Imagine you are Lewis Hines and have been traveling the country taking pictures of child labor. Write a descriptive paragraph about the working conditions you have observed.

My writing: _____

_____

_____

_____

_____

_____

_____

_____

_____

_____

DOWN WITH CHILD LABOR

Ideas Teammates Share

United States Social Studies: Engaging Cooperative Learning Activities
Kagan Publishing • 800.933.2667 • www.KaganOnline.com

161

Industrialization
The Transcontinental Railroad

■ **RallyCoach Directions:** Take turns answering each question as your partner coaches. Explain your thinking to your coach.
■ **Sage-N-Scribe Directions:** The Sage describes what he or she knows about the question so the Scribe can answer the question. The Sage and Scribe switch roles for each question.

Name _____

1. **Which president commissioned the building of a transcontinental railroad?**
   a) Andrew Jackson
   b) Abraham Lincoln
   c) Theodore Roosevelt
   d) Ulysses S. Grant

2. **What sparked the need to build a transcontinental railroad?**
   a) There was no way to deliver messages to the west coast.
   b) The Civil War was moving west beyond the Louisiana territory.
   c) News could travel fast but it still took a long time for people and goods.
   d) The president needed a way to campaign in western territories.

3. **What was the name of the act the president signed in order for the railroad to be built?**
   a) Pacific Railway Act
   b) Transcontinental Railroad Act
   c) Western Expansion Railway Act
   d) Iron Horse Railroad Act

4. **Which company hired primarily Irish immigrants, former slaves, and Civil War veterans?**
   a) Union Pacific
   b) Central Pacific
   c) Western Atlantic
   d) Southern Pacific

Name _____

1. **What were the names of the two companies commissioned by the president to build the railroad?**
   a) Union and Confederate
   b) Union Pacific and Central Pacific
   c) Western Atlantic and South Pacific
   d) Omaha and California

2. **Which of the following was NOT a problem faced when building the railroads?**
   a) It was hard to find enough workers for the huge project.
   b) Landforms in the west made building difficult.
   c) American Indians fought the building of the railroad.
   d) Funding for the railroad ran out midway through completion.

3. **One company was hired to lay the westbound tracks for the railroad. Where in the east did it begin?**
   a) Saint Louis, Missouri
   b) San Francisco, California
   c) Omaha, Nebraska
   d) Promontory, Utah

4. **What caused the death of many Chinese workers while in the Sierra Nevada mountain range?**
   a) Avalanches from the falling snow
   b) Blasting tunnels through solid rock with dynamite
   c) Attacks from American Indians
   d) Harsh cold conditions and little food

United States Social Studies: Engaging Cooperative Learning Activities
Kagan Publishing • 800.933.2667 • www.KaganOnline.com

162

Industrialization
The Spanish-American War of 1898

Directions: Copy one set of cards for each team. Cut out each card along the dotted lines. Give each team a set of cards to play Fan-N-Pick or Showdown.

1 *Industrialization*

Name two causes of the Spanish-American War.

Fan-N-Pick/Showdown

2 *Industrialization*

What territories did America gain from Spain following the war?

Fan-N-Pick/Showdown

3 *Industrialization*

What role did newspapers play in the fight of the Spanish-American War?

Fan-N-Pick/Showdown

4 *Industrialization*

Who was the president during the Spanish-American War of 1898?

Fan-N-Pick/Showdown

5 *Industrialization*

What name was given to Theodore Roosevelt's group of volunteer soldiers consisting of American Indians, cowboys, and college athletes?

Fan-N-Pick/Showdown

6 *Industrialization*

What was Theodore Roosevelt's job prior to leading the volunteer forces in Cuba?

Fan-N-Pick/Showdown

7 *Industrialization*

What event happened on the night of February 15, 1898, causing many Americans to blame the Spanish?

Fan-N-Pick/Showdown

8 *Industrialization*

What was the Spanish army's reaction to the Cuban people revolting the Spanish rule?

Fan-N-Pick/Showdown

United States Social Studies: Engaging Cooperative Learning Activities
Kagan Publishing • 800.933.2667 • www.KaganOnline.com

163

Industrialization
Equal Rights/Women's Vote

Directions: Copy one set of cards for each team. Cut out each card along the dotted lines. Give each team a set of cards to play Fan-N-Pick or Showdown.

1 *Industrialization*
What was the name of the meeting led by Lucretia Mott and Elizabeth Cady Stanton in 1848?
Fan-N-Pick/Showdown

2 *Industrialization*
What amendment, ratified in 1920, gave women the right to vote?
Fan-N-Pick/Showdown

3 *Industrialization*
What is another name, in honor of this woman's efforts for women's rights, for the amendment ratified in 1920?
Fan-N-Pick/Showdown

4 *Industrialization*
How did women's roles during World War I strengthen the issue of women's rights to vote?
Fan-N-Pick/Showdown

5 *Industrialization*
What term means "the right to vote?"
Fan-N-Pick/Showdown

6 *Industrialization*
True or False:
Before all women were allowed to vote, some states and territories allowed women to vote in state elections.
Fan-N-Pick/Showdown

7 *Industrialization*
What term is given to people who believed women deserved the right to vote?
Fan-N-Pick/Showdown

8 *Industrialization*
What did Alice Paul found that brought public attention to women's suffrage through marches, picketing, and hunger strikes?
Fan-N-Pick/Showdown

9 *Industrialization*
A huge step in women's rights was the first woman elected into Congress. Who is she?
Fan-N-Pick/Showdown

10 *Industrialization*
In addition to not being allowed to vote, what other limitations did women's rights include?
Fan-N-Pick/Showdown

Industrialization
The Rise of Unions and Labor Laws

Name: _____

Directions: Pair up and take turns circling the answer to each question. Don't forget to get your partner's initials.

Which of the following sentences best captures the working conditions of cities in the 1900s?

a) Men worked long hours in dangerous conditions while women stayed at home.
b) Children were expected to work in only desperate conditions and very rarely.
c) Men, women, and children often worked over 12 hours a day, 7 days a week in poor conditions.
d) Labor bosses treated workers fairly and supported labor unions.

_____
Initials

What was a sweatshop?

a) A place were sweats are made
b) A cramped, hot workshop, often where women operated sewing machines
c) A place where goods were offered for sale from a local sewing company
d) The location where mine workers met to receive their week's wages

_____
Initials

What is the purpose of a labor union?

a) Workers join together to fight for improved working conditions and increased wages.
b) Employers join together in order to get the best performance from employees.
c) Government agencies investigate child labor.
d) The union prevents workers from earning more than government officials.

_____
Initials

Who was Samuel Gompers?

a) A factory worker that locked the doors resulting in deaths after a fire broke out
b) A government official leading the fight against labor unions
c) A mill worker who walked out during his shift in protest of poor working conditions
d) A cigar factory worker who was one of the first union leaders who helped form the American Federation of Labor

_____
Initials

Which of the following was NOT a goal for the American Federation of Labor?

a) Holiday and vacation pay
b) Better wages
c) An 8-hour work day
d) End of child labor

_____
Initials

What holiday was recognized by Congress as a national holiday in 1894 to honor the workers and their contributions in America?

a) Flag Day
b) Spring break
c) Labor Day
d) Samuel Gompers Day

_____
Initials

United States Social Studies: Engaging Cooperative Learning Activities
Kagan Publishing • 800.933.2667 • www.KaganOnline.com

165

Industrialization
Inventions

Directions: Cut cards along the dotted lines. Distribute one card per student in sequence so for every student with an invention picture card, there is a student with a matching description card. Students use cards to play Mix-N-Match.

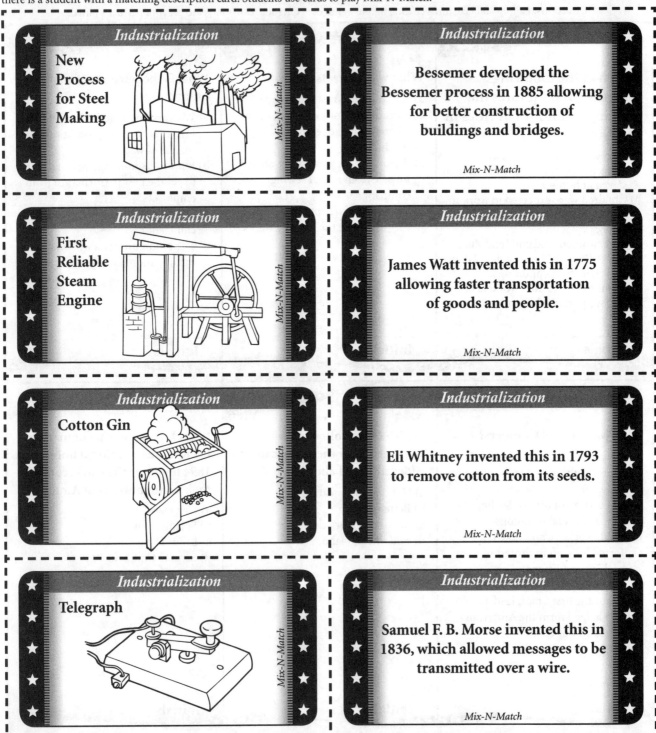

Industrialization

New Process for Steel Making

Mix-N-Match

Industrialization

Bessemer developed the Bessemer process in 1885 allowing for better construction of buildings and bridges.

Mix-N-Match

Industrialization

First Reliable Steam Engine

Mix-N-Match

Industrialization

James Watt invented this in 1775 allowing faster transportation of goods and people.

Mix-N-Match

Industrialization

Cotton Gin

Mix-N-Match

Industrialization

Eli Whitney invented this in 1793 to remove cotton from its seeds.

Mix-N-Match

Industrialization

Telegraph

Mix-N-Match

Industrialization

Samuel F. B. Morse invented this in 1836, which allowed messages to be transmitted over a wire.

Mix-N-Match

United States Social Studies: Engaging Cooperative Learning Activities
Kagan Publishing • 800.933.2667 • www.KaganOnline.com

Industrialization
Inventions

Directions: Cut cards along the dotted lines. Distribute one card per student in sequence so for every student with an invention picture card, there is a student with a matching description card. Students use cards to play Mix-N-Match.

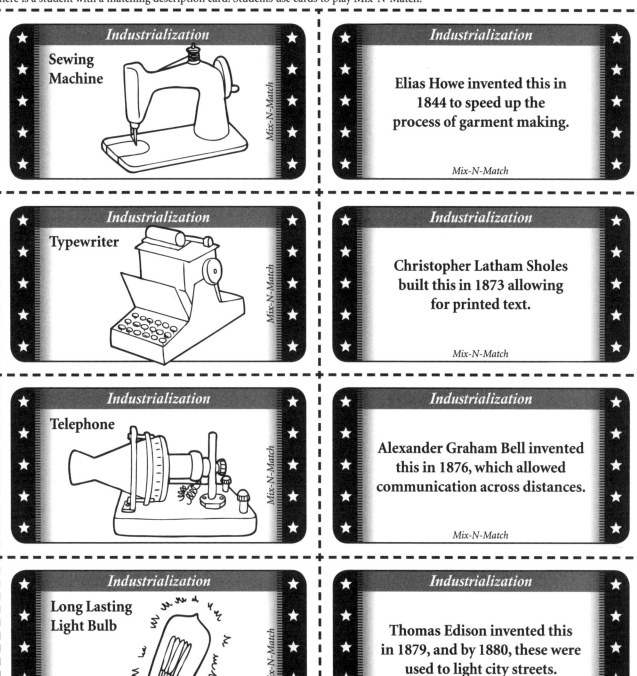

Industrialization

Sewing Machine

Mix-N-Match

Industrialization

Elias Howe invented this in 1844 to speed up the process of garment making.

Mix-N-Match

Industrialization

Typewriter

Mix-N-Match

Industrialization

Christopher Latham Sholes built this in 1873 allowing for printed text.

Mix-N-Match

Industrialization

Telephone

Mix-N-Match

Industrialization

Alexander Graham Bell invented this in 1876, which allowed communication across distances.

Mix-N-Match

Industrialization

Long Lasting Light Bulb

Mix-N-Match

Industrialization

Thomas Edison invented this in 1879, and by 1880, these were used to light city streets.

Mix-N-Match

United States Social Studies: Engaging Cooperative Learning Activities
Kagan Publishing • 800.933.2667 • www.KaganOnline.com

167

Industrialization
Inventions

Directions: Cut cards along the dotted lines. Distribute one card per student in sequence so for every student with an invention picture card, there is a student with a matching description card. Students use cards to play Mix-N-Match.

United States Social Studies: Engaging Cooperative Learning Activities
Kagan Publishing • 800.933.2667 • www.KaganOnline.com

World War I

Cooperative Learning Activities

World War I
The League of Nations

Directions: Think about the prompt, and then write your own response. When done, RoundRobin share your writing with your teammates. Use the space at the bottom to record ideas your teammates share.

Prompt: The League of Nations was created to prevent future wars but was a failure for multiple reasons. In your opinion, what was the major reason the League of Nations was unsuccessful? Explain.

My writing: _____

_____

_____

_____

_____

_____

_____

_____

_____

_____

Ideas Teammates Share

United States Social Studies: Engaging Cooperative Learning Activities
Kagan Publishing • 800.933.2667 • www.KaganOnline.com

World War I
The Treaty of Versailles

Directions: Think about the prompt, and then write your own response. When done, RoundRobin share your writing with your teammates. Use the space at the bottom to record ideas your teammates share.

Prompt: How might the world be different had the Treaty of Versailles not been created? Explain your thinking.

My writing: _____

_____

_____

_____

_____

_____

_____

_____

_____

_____

_____

BIG FOUR MEET AT VERSAILLES

Ideas Teammates Share

United States Social Studies: Engaging Cooperative Learning Activities
Kagan Publishing • 800.933.2667 • www.KaganOnline.com

171

World War I
Equal Rights / Women's Suffrage

Directions: Think about the prompt, and then write your own response. When done, RoundRobin share your writing with your teammates. Use the space at the bottom to record ideas your teammates share.

Prompt: How did women's roles during World War I provide support for women gaining the right to vote?

My writing: _____

_____

_____

_____

_____

_____

_____

_____

_____

_____

Ideas Teammates Share

World War I
Impact of Trench Warfare

Directions: Think about the prompt, and then write your own response. When done, RoundRobin share your writing with your teammates. Use the space at the bottom to record ideas your teammates share.

Prompt: Trench Warfare was a new military strategy used by both sides during World War I. Describe the impact of the trenches in defense and how it aided in the advancement in the war.

My writing: _____

_____

_____

_____

_____

_____

_____

_____

_____

_____

_____

_____

Ideas Teammates Share

United States Social Studies: Engaging Cooperative Learning Activities
Kagan Publishing • 800.933.2667 • www.KaganOnline.com

173

World War I
Treaties and Alliances

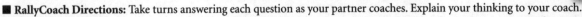

■ **RallyCoach Directions:** Take turns answering each question as your partner coaches. Explain your thinking to your coach.
■ **Sage-N-Scribe Directions:** The Sage describes what he or she knows about the question so the Scribe can answer the question. The Sage and Scribe switch roles for each question.

Name _____

1. **What was the name of the alliance between Britain, France, and Russia?**
   a) Central Powers
   b) Allied Powers
   c) North Atlantic Treaty Organization
   d) World Power Treaty

2. **What new weapon proved more deadly and caused blistered skin and burned lungs?**
   a) Automatic weapons
   b) Poison gas
   c) Long range missiles
   d) Submarine tanks

3. **Who was the President when the United States entered World War I?**
   a) Theodore Roosevelt
   b) Andrew Jackson
   c) Dwight D. Eisenhower
   d) Woodrow Wilson

4. **What is the purpose of the League of Nations?**
   a) To keep Central Powers from reforming their alliance
   b) To punish the Central Powers for years to come
   c) Act as an international organization to prevent wars
   d) Act as a balance of powers between the United States and Russia

Name _____

1. **What was the name of the alliance between Germany, Austria-Hungary, and Turkey?**
   a) Central Powers
   b) Allied Powers
   c) North Atlantic Treaty Organization
   d) World Power Treaty

2. **Which invention, along with a few modifications, changed how the war was fought?**
   a) The airplanes fought in the air and dropped bombs.
   b) The railroad brought supplies long distances.
   c) The cotton gin provided clothing and repairs faster.
   d) The television transmitted news reports.

3. **What national holiday is celebrated on November 11th in honor of those who fought in wars and is also the date the Central Powers surrendered?**
   a) Labor Day
   b) Veterans Day
   c) Memorial Day
   d) Flag Day

4. **Why did the United States Senate refuse to approve the Treaty of Versailles or join the League?**
   a) They did not want to be forced into future wars.
   b) President Wilson did not agree with the League.
   c) The Allied Powers lost the war and were not allowed to join the League.
   d) The leaders could not agree on a future meeting date to finalize the details.

174

United States Social Studies: Engaging Cooperative Learning Activities
Kagan Publishing • 800.933.2667 • www.KaganOnline.com

World War I
War Strategies

Directions: Copy one set of cards for each team. Cut out each card along the dotted lines. Give each team a set of cards to play Fan-N-Pick or Showdown.

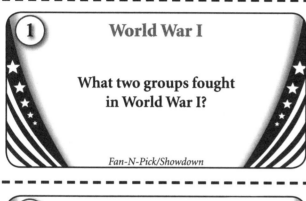

1 — World War I

What two groups fought in World War I?

Fan-N-Pick/Showdown

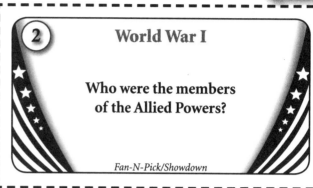

2 — World War I

Who were the members of the Allied Powers?

Fan-N-Pick/Showdown

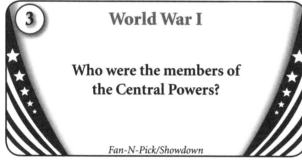

3 — World War I

Who were the members of the Central Powers?

Fan-N-Pick/Showdown

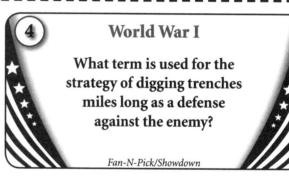

4 — World War I

What term is used for the strategy of digging trenches miles long as a defense against the enemy?

Fan-N-Pick/Showdown

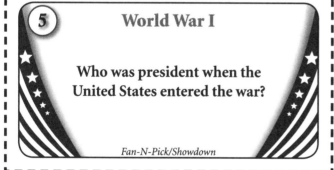

5 — World War I

Who was president when the United States entered the war?

Fan-N-Pick/Showdown

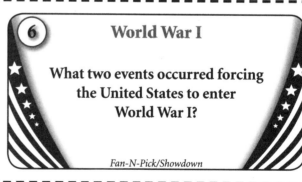

6 — World War I

What two events occurred forcing the United States to enter World War I?

Fan-N-Pick/Showdown

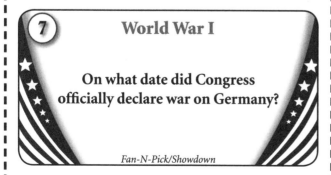

7 — World War I

On what date did Congress officially declare war on Germany?

Fan-N-Pick/Showdown

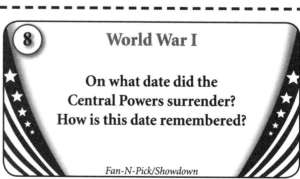

8 — World War I

On what date did the Central Powers surrender? How is this date remembered?

Fan-N-Pick/Showdown

United States Social Studies: Engaging Cooperative Learning Activities
Kagan Publishing • 800.933.2667 • www.KaganOnline.com

175

World War I
War Strategies

Directions: Copy one set of cards for each team. Cut out each card along the dotted lines. Give each team a set of cards to play Fan-N-Pick or Showdown.

9 World War I

What was the name of the proposed organization to prevent future wars?

Fan-N-Pick/Showdown

10 World War I

What officially ended World War I?

Fan-N-Pick/Showdown

11 World War I

Why did the United States refuse to join the League of Nations or approve the Treaty of Versailles?

Fan-N-Pick/Showdown

12 World War I

Woodrow Wilson gave a speech to Congress in 1918 with a plan for peace and an end to World War I. What is this speech known as?

Fan-N-Pick/Showdown

13 World War I

Fan-N-Pick/Showdown

14 World War I

Fan-N-Pick/Showdown

15 World War I

Fan-N-Pick/Showdown

16 World War I

Fan-N-Pick/Showdown

United States Social Studies: Engaging Cooperative Learning Activities
Kagan Publishing • 800.933.2667 • www.KaganOnline.com

World War I
Powers of War

Directions: Copy cards, one per student. Cut out each card along the dotted lines and follow the directions for Who Am I?

1 — World War I

Alliance

Who Am I?

2 — World War I

Allied Powers

Who Am I?

3 — World War I

Central Powers

Who Am I?

4 — World War I

Trench

Who Am I?

United States Social Studies: Engaging Cooperative Learning Activities
Kagan Publishing • 800.933.2667 • www.KaganOnline.com

177

World War I
Powers of War

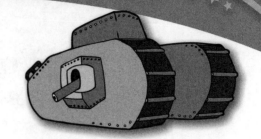

Directions: Copy cards, one per student. Cut out each card along the dotted lines and follow the directions for Who Am I?

5 *World War I*

Britain

Who Am I?

6 *World War I*

France

Who Am I?

7 *World War I*

Russia

Who Am I?

8 *World War I*

Germany

Who Am I?

178

United States Social Studies: Engaging Cooperative Learning Activities
Kagan Publishing • 800.933.2667 • www.KaganOnline.com

World War I
Powers of War

Directions: Copy cards, one per student. Cut out each card along the dotted lines and follow the directions for Who Am I?

9 *World War I*

Turkey

Who Am I?

10 *World War I*

League of Nations

Who Am I?

11 *World War I*

Treaty of Versailles

Who Am I?

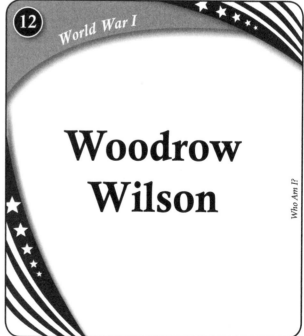

12 *World War I*

Woodrow Wilson

Who Am I?

United States Social Studies: Engaging Cooperative Learning Activities
Kagan Publishing • 800.933.2667 • www.KaganOnline.com

179

World War I
Powers of War

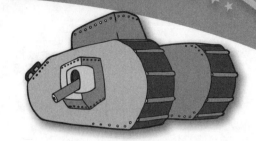

Directions: Copy cards, one per student. Cut out each card along the dotted lines and follow the directions for Who Am I?

13 — *World War I*

Austria-Hungary

Who Am I?

14 — *World War I*

Meuse-Argonne Offensive

Who Am I?

15 — *World War I*

Isolationism

Who Am I?

16 — *World War I*

Who Am I?

180

United States Social Studies: Engaging Cooperative Learning Activities
Kagan Publishing • 800.933.2667 • www.KaganOnline.com

World War I
War Tactics

Directions: The class "mixes" until the teacher calls, "pair." Students find a new partner to discuss or answer the teacher's question.

---

① *World War I*

How did technology change the way World War I was fought compared to previous wars?

Mix-Pair-Share

---

② *World War I*

What role did trenches, or trench warfare, play in the military strategy on both sides?

Mix-Pair-Share

---

③ *World War I*

In your opinion, what was the greatest cause of America joining the fight against the Central Powers: an intercepted telegraph from Germany to Mexico promising help to get back lands lost to the U.S.; or German submarines sinking American submarines? Explain.

Mix-Pair-Share

---

④ *World War I*

Was the decision of the United States to enter World War I justified? Explain your thinking.

Mix-Pair-Share

---

⑤ *World War I*

How might the war have been different had the United States chosen not to fight against the Central Powers? Justify your reasoning.

Mix-Pair-Share

---

⑥ *World War I*

How might our world be different today had the Allied Powers not won the war against the Central Powers?

Mix-Pair-Share

United States Social Studies: Engaging Cooperative Learning Activities
Kagan Publishing • 800.933.2667 • www.KaganOnline.com

181

World War I
War Tactics

Directions: The class "mixes" until the teacher calls, "pair." Students find a new partner to discuss or answer the teacher's question.

---

7 *World War I*

Sequence the major events of World War I starting with before the United States joined the war until the signing of the Treaty of Versailles.

Mix-Pair-Share

---

8 *World War I*

How might history have been different had the United States Senate decided to join the League of Nations? Explain.

Mix-Pair-Share

---

9 *World War I*

Following the war, Germany was forbidden to have submarines, aircraft, armored cars, or tanks in order to prevent starting another war. Was this an effective strategy? Explain.

Mix-Pair-Share

---

10 *World War I*

Was the League of Nations a successful or unsuccessful joining of world powers? Justify your thinking.

Mix-Pair-Share

---

11 *World War I*

Mix-Pair-Share

---

12 *World War I*

Mix-Pair-Share

Depression

Cooperative Learning Activities

The Great Depression
Causes

Directions: Think about the prompt, and then write your own response. When done, RoundRobin share your writing with your teammates. Use the space at the bottom to record ideas your teammates share.

Prompt

In your opinion, what action was the greatest cause of the Great Depression? Justify your answer with examples from history.

My Writing

_____

_____

_____

_____

_____

_____

_____

_____

_____

_____

_____

Ideas Teammates Share

United States Social Studies: Engaging Cooperative Learning Activities
Kagan Publishing • 800.933.2667 • www.KaganOnline.com

The Great Depression
Franklin D. Roosevelt

Directions: Think about the prompt, and then write your own response. When done, RoundRobin share your writing with your teammates. Use the space at the bottom to record ideas your teammates share.

Prompt

Franklin D. Roosevelt was sworn into office in 1933. During his inaugural speech, he said, *"The only thing we have to fear is fear itself."* How does this phrase summarize Franklin D. Roosevelt's presidency?

My Writing

Ideas Teammates Share

United States Social Studies: Engaging Cooperative Learning Activities
Kagan Publishing • 800.933.2667 • www.KaganOnline.com

185

The Great Depression
Economic Conditions

■ **RallyCoach Directions:** Take turns answering each question as your partner coaches. Explain your thinking to your coach.
■ **Sage-N-Scribe Directions:** The Sage describes what he or she knows about the question so the Scribe can answer the question. The Sage and Scribe switch roles for each question.

Name _____

1. **What bank action was a cause for the Great Depression?**
   a) Banks were careless with loans as people could not pay loans back.
   b) People invested money into stock markets.
   c) Banks did not provide loans to struggling businesses.
   d) Banks made more goods than could be sold.

2. **What was NOT a result of having a surplus of goods or crops in the 1920s?**
   a) Prices of foods and goods increased.
   b) Factories began laying off people.
   c) Unemployment rose.
   d) Fewer people could afford to buy new products.

3. **What name was given to Franklin D. Roosevelt's series of programs to improve the economy?**
   a) The New Deal
   b) Roosevelt Plan
   c) FDR Inaugural Deal
   d) Great Depression Revitalization Program

4. **What was the result of the Social Security Act passed in 1935?**
   a) To allow citizens to work in jobs that best suited individual interests
   b) To employ large numbers of unemployed young men in forestry work
   c) To provide pay to the unemployed and elderly funded by taxes of employers and employees
   d) To provide security for docks and ports to protect American trade

Name _____

1. **What event, in 1929, was the beginning of the Great Depression?**
   a) Stock Market Crash
   b) Black Friday
   c) Implementation of Unemployment Benefits
   d) Raising of the minimum wage

2. **What was a result of farmers being unable to pay off their debts?**
   a) Farmers went on strike for government help.
   b) Banks took ownership of farms to help recover their loss in loans given.
   c) Food prices soared in order to pay off debts.
   d) Farmers had to relocate to new farms.

3. **What was NOT a goal of Franklin D. Roosevelt when he took office in 1933?**
   a) To assist those without work or homes
   b) To help the nation's economy recover
   c) To promote overseas trades to offer Americans work
   d) To reform conditions of the Great Depression

4. **What was the result of the Civilian Conservation Corps (CCC)?**
   a) Only the strongest men and women could work in outdoor elements.
   b) Civilians may join national forces to pay off debts.
   c) A program offered solutions to recycling while employing factory workers in the industry.
   d) Over 3 million young men were employed to work in forests and natural resources on environmental projects.

United States Social Studies: Engaging Cooperative Learning Activities
Kagan Publishing • 800.933.2667 • www.KaganOnline.com

186

The Great Depression
Events of the Crash

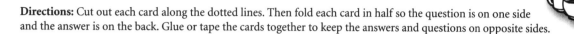

Directions: Cut out each card along the dotted lines. Then fold each card in half so the question is on one side and the answer is on the back. Glue or tape the cards together to keep the answers and questions on opposite sides.

 ① The Great Depression

What event is known to have caused the Great Depression?

a) The beginning of World War I
b) The end of the Great Awakening
c) The Stock Market Crash of 1929
d) The end of slavery

Quiz-Quiz-Trade • Question

① The Great Depression

What event is known to have caused the Great Depression?

c) The Stock Market Crash of 1929

Quiz-Quiz-Trade • Answer

② The Great Depression

Which of the following was NOT a result of the Stock Market Crash of 1929?

a) Businesses went bankrupt.
b) More than 12 million people lost their jobs.
c) Workers earned less money in their jobs.
d) More banks were created to offer loans.

Quiz-Quiz-Trade • Question

② The Great Depression

Which of the following was NOT a result of the Stock Market Crash of 1929?

d) More banks were created to offer loans.

Quiz-Quiz-Trade • Answer

③ The Great Depression

Which of the following was NOT a cause of the Great Depression?

a) More people invested money in risky stocks and deals.
b) Businesses were producing fewer goods than they could sell.
c) People took out loans they could not repay.
d) Machines were replacing jobs normally held by people.

Quiz-Quiz-Trade • Question

③ The Great Depression

Which of the following was NOT a cause of the Great Depression?

b) Business were producing fewer goods than they could sell

Quiz-Quiz-Trade • Answer

United States Social Studies: Engaging Cooperative Learning Activities
Kagan Publishing • 800.933.2667 • www.KaganOnline.com

187

The Great Depression
Events of the Crash

Directions: Cut out each card along the dotted lines. Then fold each card in half so the question is on one side and the answer is on the back. Glue or tape the cards together to keep the answers and questions on opposite sides.

---

④ The Great Depression

Which sentence best summarizes life prior to the Great Depression, also known as the Roaring Twenties?

a) Women were forced to go to work to support growing families.

b) Henry Ford's assembly line slowed down work production.

c) An economic boom occurred resulting in higher wages and shorter work weeks.

d) People were reluctant to take bank loans due to mistrust.

Quiz-Quiz-Trade • Question

---

④ The Great Depression

Which sentence best summarizes life prior to the Great Depression, also known as the Roaring Twenties?

a) Women were forced to go to work to support growing families.

Quiz-Quiz-Trade • Answer

---

⑤ The Great Depression

What time frame did the Great Depression occur?

a) 1929 to 1939

b) 1920 to 1940

c) 1925 to 1935

d) 1924 to 1936

Quiz-Quiz-Trade • Question

---

⑤ The Great Depression

What time frame did the Great Depression occur?

a) 1929 to 1939

Quiz-Quiz-Trade • Answer

---

⑥ The Great Depression

What sentence best describes the stock market?

a) A place you can go to buy goods such as cattle

b) An economic system that allows people to buy and sell shares of businesses

c) An imaginary business where thieves take someone's money

d) A place that sells stockings and other goods

Quiz-Quiz-Trade • Question

---

⑥ The Great Depression

What sentence best describes the stock market?

b) An economic system that allows people to buy and sell shares of businesses

Quiz-Quiz-Trade • Answer

United States Social Studies: Engaging Cooperative Learning Activities
Kagan Publishing • 800.933.2667 • www.KaganOnline.com

188

The Great Depression
Events of the Crash

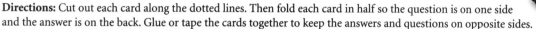

Directions: Cut out each card along the dotted lines. Then fold each card in half so the question is on one side and the answer is on the back. Glue or tape the cards together to keep the answers and questions on opposite sides.

---

7 The Great Depression

What term is often used to describe the day the stock market crashed?

a) D Day
b) Black Friday
c) Stock Day
d) Black Tuesday

Quiz-Quiz-Trade • Question

---

7 The Great Depression

What term is often used to describe the day the stock market crashed?

d) Black Tuesday

Quiz-Quiz-Trade • Answer

---

8 The Great Depression

What was the name of the legislation Franklin D. Roosevelt passed to help the country during the Great Depression?

a) Franklin's Deal
b) The Great Depression Reform Act
c) The New Deal
d) American Job Growth Act

Quiz-Quiz-Trade • Question

---

8 The Great Depression

What was the name of the legislation Franklin D. Roosevelt passed to help the country during the Great Depression?

c) The New Deal

Quiz-Quiz-Trade • Answer

---

9 The Great Depression

Which of the following was NOT a goal of the New Deal?
a) Help the jobless and the poor receive work
b) Help the economy recover
c) Heavily tax the wealthy
d) Improve work conditions

Quiz-Quiz-Trade • Question

---

9 The Great Depression

Which of the following was NOT a goal of the New Deal?

c) Heavily tax the wealthy

Quiz-Quiz-Trade • Answer

United States Social Studies: Engaging Cooperative Learning Activities
Kagan Publishing • 800.933.2667 • www.KaganOnline.com

189

The Great Depression
Events of the Crash

Directions: Cut out each card along the dotted lines. Then fold each card in half so the question is on one side and the answer is on the back. Glue or tape the cards together to keep the answers and questions on opposite sides.

---

10 **The Great Depression**

What was the Civilian Conservation Corps (CCC)?

a) Concentration work camps set up for debtors
b) Camps of young men who worked to conserve forests and natural resources
c) A group of men hired to travel to collect unpaid debts
d) A group of men hired to visit homes and offer money conservation tips to debtors

Quiz-Quiz-Trade • Question

---

10 **The Great Depression**

What was the Civilian Conservation Corps (CCC)?

b) Camps of young men who worked to conserve forests and natural resources

Quiz-Quiz-Trade • Answer

---

11 **The Great Depression**

What was the name of the act passed in 1935 which provided payments to those unemployed and to the elderly?

a) Health Care Act
b) Care and Compassion Act
c) Unemployment Act
d) Social Security Act

Quiz-Quiz-Trade • Question

---

11 **The Great Depression**

What was the name of the act passed in 1935 which provided payments to those unemployed and to the elderly?

d) Social Security Act

Quiz-Quiz-Trade • Answer

---

12 **The Great Depression**

What is the term given to the period of severe drought in the Great Plains?

a) Drought Days
b) Dust Bowl
c) Rain Away
d) Economic Down Turn

Quiz-Quiz-Trade • Question

---

12 **The Great Depression**

What is the term given to the period of severe drought in the Great Plains?

b) Dust Bowl

Quiz-Quiz-Trade • Answer

190

United States Social Studies: Engaging Cooperative Learning Activities
Kagan Publishing • 800.933.2667 • www.KaganOnline.com

The Great Depression
Events of the Crash

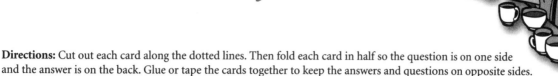

Directions: Cut out each card along the dotted lines. Then fold each card in half so the question is on one side and the answer is on the back. Glue or tape the cards together to keep the answers and questions on opposite sides.

 13 The Great Depression

What event in 1941 helped end the period known as the Great Depression?

a) World War II
b) Vietnam War
c) World War I
d) Civil Rights Movement

Quiz-Quiz-Trade • Question

 13 The Great Depression

What event in 1941 helped end the period known as the Great Depression?

a) World War II

Quiz-Quiz-Trade • Answer

 14 The Great Depression

In what way did World War II help the economy recover?

a) Created high wages for military officers
b) Created jobs to build war supplies
c) Forced women to remain home rather than to work
d) Prevented the use of assembly lines and machines

Quiz-Quiz-Trade • Question

 14 The Great Depression

In what way did World War II help the economy recover?

b) Created jobs to build war supplies

Quiz-Quiz-Trade • Answer

 15 The Great Depression

What is the term given for government-imposed restrictions on items such as butter and gasoline in order to preserve supplies?

a) Tariffs
b) Aids
c) Rations
d) Taxes

Quiz-Quiz-Trade • Question

 15 The Great Depression

What is the term given for government-imposed restrictions on items such as butter and gasoline in order to preserve supplies?

c) Rations

Quiz-Quiz-Trade • Answer

United States Social Studies: Engaging Cooperative Learning Activities
Kagan Publishing • 800.933.2667 • www.KaganOnline.com

191

The Great Depression
Life Before and During the Great Depression

Directions: The class "mixes" until the teacher calls, "pair." Students find a new partner to discuss or answer the teacher's question.

---

①

The Great Depression

How did the average person's life change from 1920 and the "Roaring Twenties" to 1939 and the end of the Great Depression?

Mix-Pair-Share

---

②

The Great Depression

In your opinion, who suffered the greatest during the Great Depression: farmers or factory workers? Explain your thinking.

Mix-Pair-Share

---

③

The Great Depression

Which aspect of President Roosevelt's New Deal had the greatest impact on the country? Explain your reasoning.

Mix-Pair-Share

---

④

The Great Depression

Imagine you had the ability to travel back in time to the Great Depression. What help or assistance would you provide to those in need and why? Explain your thinking.

Mix-Pair-Share

---

⑤

The Great Depression

In your opinion, what was harder for farmers: inability to pay debts to banks during the Great Depression or the Dust Bowl over the plains? Justify your thinking.

Mix-Pair-Share

---

⑥

The Great Depression

In your opinion, did President Roosevelt make good decisions during the Great Depression? Support your position with examples from history.

Mix-Pair-Share

---

⑦

The Great Depression

Describe some of the assistance programs offered to those in need during the Great Depression. What else could have been done to help families in need? Explain.

Mix-Pair-Share

---

⑧

The Great Depression

Describe the life for a child during the Great Depression. How is this different from or similar to your own life? Explain.

Mix-Pair-Share

192

United States Social Studies: Engaging Cooperative Learning Activities
Kagan Publishing • 800.933.2667 • www.KaganOnline.com

World War II

Cooperative Learning Activities

World War II
Bombing of Pearl Harbor

Directions: Think about the prompt, and then write your own response. When done, RoundRobin share your writing with your teammates. Use the space at the bottom to record ideas your teammates share.

Prompt: Describe the impact that the bombing of Pearl Harbor had on Americans in the past and in the present.

My writing: _____

_____

_____

_____

_____

_____

_____

_____

_____

_____

_____

Ideas Teammates Share

194

United States Social Studies: Engaging Cooperative Learning Activities
Kagan Publishing • 800.933.2667 • www.KaganOnline.com

World War II
World War II Newscast

Directions: Think about the prompt, and then write your own response. When done, RoundRobin share your writing with your teammates. Use the space at the bottom to record ideas your teammates share.

Prompt: Many people listened to the radio during the 1930s. Imagine you are a radio newscaster and have just heard the news of a war in Europe, later known as World War II. Write a newscast report sharing information on the events current to the period.

My writing: _____

_____
_____
_____
_____
_____
_____
_____
_____
_____
_____
_____

Ideas Teammates Share

United States Social Studies: Engaging Cooperative Learning Activities
Kagan Publishing • 800.933.2667 • www.KaganOnline.com

195

World War II
Allies and Enemies

Name: _____

Directions: Pair up and take turns circling the answer to each question. Don't forget to get your partner's initials.

1

Who was the leader of the Nazi Party in Germany?
a) Benito Mussolini
b) Adolf Hitler
c) Joseph Stalin
d) Dwight D. Eisenhower

_____
Initials

2

What country did the Italian dictator invade in 1935 in hopes to make it an Italian colony?
a) Germany
b) Austria
c) Ethiopia
d) Czechoslovakia

_____
Initials

3

Which of the following was NOT part of the alliance known as the Axis?
a) Italy
b) Germany
c) Japan
d) France

_____
Initials

4

Which event sparked the beginning of World War II?
a) Hitler sent troops into Poland.
b) Japan invaded China.
c) Germany invaded Austria.
d) Britain and France joined in an alliance known as the Allies.

_____
Initials

5

What action resulted in Joseph Stalin joining the Allies?
a) The Soviet Union began protesting the war.
b) Hitler broke a pact and attacked the Soviet Union.
c) Japan bombed Pearl Harbor.
d) Germany began building concentration camps.

_____
Initials

6

What happened on December 7, 1941, that forced the United States into the war?
a) Bombing of Pearl Harbor
b) Joseph Stalin joined the Allies
c) Hitler declared war on Poland
d) Japan joined the Axis with Germany

_____
Initials

7

Which of the following was NOT a result of the United States joining the Allies?
a) Women took men's places in factories.
b) Car manufactures began making tanks and planes.
c) Military uniforms were produced by clothing companies.
d) Protestors protested the war resulting in lower sense of patriotism

_____
Initials

8

What was the result of Roosevelt's Executive Order #9066 concerning Japanese Americans?
a) Japanese Americans were asked to spy against Japan.
b) Japanese Americans on the West Coast were placed in relocation camps.
c) Japanese Americans were tried for treason and jailed.
d) Japanese Americans were forced to give up American citizenship and return to Japan.

_____
Initials

9

Who was the American Army General during the invasion of Normandy?
a) Dwight D. Eisenhower
b) Franklin D. Roosevelt
c) Harry S. Truman
d) Bonito Mussolini

_____
Initials

United States Social Studies: *Engaging Cooperative Learning Activities*
Kagan Publishing • 800.933.2667 • www.KaganOnline.com

196

World War II
The Holocaust

Directions: Copy one set of cards for each team. Cut out each card along the dotted lines. Give each team a set of cards to play Fan-N-Pick or Showdown.

1 *World War II*

Name two groups of people Adolf Hitler targeted during the period known as the Holocaust.

Fan-N-Pick/Showdown

2 *World War II*

What term is used to describe the prisons where Jews and others were sent who opposed Hitler's rule?

Fan-N-Pick/Showdown

3 *World War II*

What is the name of the group led by Adolf Hitler?

Fan-N-Pick/Showdown

4 *World War II*

What did Adolf Hitler and the Nazis hope to achieve by the widespread killing of Jews and others considered as enemies?

Fan-N-Pick/Showdown

5 *World War II*

Approximately how many Jewish people were killed during the Holocaust period?

Fan-N-Pick/Showdown

6 *World War II*

Name two ways Jewish people tried to escape capture from the Nazis.

Fan-N-Pick/Showdown

7 *World War II*

Which two countries were termed the world's "superpowers" following World War II?

Fan-N-Pick/Showdown

8 *World War II*

What organization was formed in order to work together to find peaceful solutions for international problems?

Fan-N-Pick/Showdown

United States Social Studies: *Engaging Cooperative Learning Activities*
Kagan Publishing • 800.933.2667 • www.KaganOnline.com

197

World War II
Events Surrounding the War

Directions: Cut out each card along the dotted lines. Then fold each card in half so the question is on one side and the answer is on the back. Glue or tape the cards together to keep the answers and questions on opposite sides.

World War II

1

What term is given to the leader of a country who has complete control over their people?

Quiz-Quiz-Trade • Question

World War II

1

What term is given to the leader of a country who has complete control over his people?

A dictator

Quiz-Quiz-Trade • Answer

World War II

2

Who was the head of the Germany's Nazi Party during World War II?

Quiz-Quiz-Trade • Question

World War II

2

Who was the head of the Germany's Nazi Party during World War II?

Adolf Hilter

Quiz-Quiz-Trade • Answer

World War II

3

Who were the majority of people targeted by Hitler's hatred?

Quiz-Quiz-Trade • Question

World War II

3

Who were the majority of people targeted by Hitler's hatred?

Jews

Quiz-Quiz-Trade • Answer

World War II

4

In addition to Germany, what other two nations joined forces to form the alliance known as Axis?

Quiz-Quiz-Trade • Question

World War II

4

In addition to Germany, what other two nations joined forces to form the alliance known as Axis?

Italy and Japan

Quiz-Quiz-Trade • Answer

198

United States Social Studies: Engaging Cooperative Learning Activities
Kagan Publishing • 800.933.2667 • www.KaganOnline.com

World War II
Events Surrounding the War

Directions: Cut out each card along the dotted lines. Then fold each card in half so the question is on one side and the answer is on the back. Glue or tape the cards together to keep the answers and questions on opposite sides.

---

⑤ *World War II*

What countries joined the alliance known as the Allies?

Quiz-Quiz-Trade • Question

---

⑤ *World War II*

What countries joined the alliance known as the Allies?
Britain and France

Quiz-Quiz-Trade • Answer

---

⑥ *World War II*

What event caused Britain and France to declare war on Germany?

Quiz-Quiz-Trade • Question

---

⑥ *World War II*

What event caused Britain and France to declare war on Germany?
Hitler sent troops into Poland

Quiz-Quiz-Trade • Answer

---

⑦ *World War II*

Who was the dictator of the Soviet Union during World War II?

Quiz-Quiz-Trade • Question

---

⑦ *World War II*

Who was the dictator of the Soviet Union during World War II?
Joseph Stalin

Quiz-Quiz-Trade • Answer

---

⑧ *World War II*

Who was the President of the United States when the United States entered World War II in 1941?

Quiz-Quiz-Trade • Question

---

⑧ *World War II*

Who was the President of the United States when the United States entered World War II in 1941?
President Franklin D. Roosevelt

Quiz-Quiz-Trade • Answer

United States Social Studies: *Engaging Cooperative Learning Activities*
Kagan Publishing • 800.933.2667 • www.KaganOnline.com

199

World War II
Events Surrounding the War

Directions: Cut out each card along the dotted lines. Then fold each card in half so the question is on one side and the answer is on the back. Glue or tape the cards together to keep the answers and questions on opposite sides.

---

9 *World War II*

What was the date of the attack on Pearl Harbor?

Quiz-Quiz-Trade • Question

---

9 *World War II*

What was the date of the attack on Pearl Harbor?
December 7, 1941

Quiz-Quiz-Trade • Answer

---

10 *World War II*

What event caused the United States to declare war on Japan?

Quiz-Quiz-Trade • Question

---

10 *World War II*

What event caused the United States to declare war on Japan?
The attack on Pearl Harbor

Quiz-Quiz-Trade • Answer

---

11 *World War II*

Which alliance did the United States join?

Quiz-Quiz-Trade • Question

---

11 *World War II*

Which alliance did the United States join?
Allies

Quiz-Quiz-Trade • Answer

---

12 *World War II*

What did President Roosevelt's Executive Order #9066 allow?

Quiz-Quiz-Trade • Question

---

12 *World War II*

What did President Roosevelt's Executive Order #9066 allow?
Military removal of anyone seen as a threat to the United States

Quiz-Quiz-Trade • Answer

200

United States Social Studies: Engaging Cooperative Learning Activities
Kagan Publishing • 800.933.2667 • www.KaganOnline.com

World War II
Events Surrounding the War

Directions: Cut out each card along the dotted lines. Then fold each card in half so the question is on one side and the answer is on the back. Glue or tape the cards together to keep the answers and questions on opposite sides.

World War II

13

What term is given to the place where imprisoned Jews were unfairly treated and often murdered?

Quiz-Quiz-Trade • Question

World War II

13

What term is given to the place where imprisoned Jews were unfairly treated and often murdered?

Concentration Camps

Quiz-Quiz-Trade • Answer

World War II

14

What term means "widespread destruction" and refers to the murder of more than 6 million Jews during World War II?

Quiz-Quiz-Trade • Question

World War II

14

What term means "widespread destruction" and refers to the murder of more than 6 million Jews during World War II?

Holocaust

Quiz-Quiz-Trade • Answer

World War II

15

What famous event began on June 6, 1944?

Quiz-Quiz-Trade • Question

World War II

15

What famous event began on June 6, 1944?

D-Day or the Invasion of Normandy

Quiz-Quiz-Trade • Answer

World War II

16

Who was the American Army General who led the attack on Normandy, France?

Quiz-Quiz-Trade • Question

World War II

16

Who was the American Army General who led the attack on Normandy, France?

Dwight D. Eisenhower

Quiz-Quiz-Trade • Answer

United States Social Studies: Engaging Cooperative Learning Activities
Kagan Publishing • 800.933.2667 • www.KaganOnline.com

201

World War II
Events Surrounding the War

Directions: Cut out each card along the dotted lines. Then fold each card in half so the question is on one side and the answer is on the back. Glue or tape the cards together to keep the answers and questions on opposite sides.

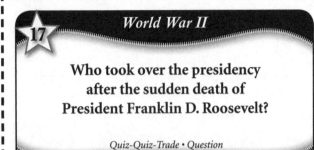

World War II

17

Who took over the presidency after the sudden death of President Franklin D. Roosevelt?

Quiz-Quiz-Trade • Question

World War II

17

Who took over the presidency after the sudden death of President Franklin Roosevelt?

Harry S. Truman

Quiz-Quiz-Trade • Answer

World War II

18

What event eventually led to the surrendering of Japan on August 14, 1945?

Quiz-Quiz-Trade • Question

World War II

18

What event eventually led to the surrendering of Japan on August 14, 1945?

The atomic bombing of Hiroshima

Quiz-Quiz-Trade • Answer

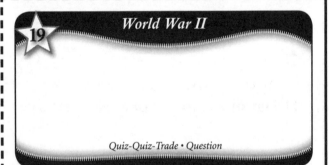

World War II

19

Quiz-Quiz-Trade • Question

World War II

19

Quiz-Quiz-Trade • Answer

World War II

20

Quiz-Quiz-Trade • Question

World War II

20

Quiz-Quiz-Trade • Answer

202

United States Social Studies: Engaging Cooperative Learning Activities
Kagan Publishing • 800.933.2667 • www.KaganOnline.com

World War II
Leaders of War

Directions: The class "mixes" until the teacher calls, "pair." Students find a new partner to discuss or answer the teacher's question.

---

1 *World War II*

How did the bombing of Pearl Harbor change America's viewpoints on the war in Europe? Explain.

Mix-Pair-Share

---

2 *World War II*

Do you think America would have joined the Allies had Japan not bombed America's Pearl Harbor? Explain.

Mix-Pair-Share

---

3 *World War II*

Was President Roosevelt and Congress justified in forcing Japanese Americans from the West Coast to go to relocation camps? Explain.

Mix-Pair-Share

---

4 *World War II*

Describe the impact women had on the war effort.

Mix-Pair-Share

---

5 *World War II*

How did the economy change during World War II following the Great Depression? Explain.

Mix-Pair-Share

---

6 *World War II*

What impact did the radio have on America during World War II? Explain.

Mix-Pair-Share

---

7 *World War II*

How did Adolf Hitler's beliefs lead to the Holocaust? What impact did this have on history? Explain.

Mix-Pair-Share

---

8 *World War II*

In what ways was the Holocaust similar to the enslavement of African slaves. Explain.

Mix-Pair-Share

---

9 *World War II*

In what ways was the Holocaust different from the enslavement of African slaves? Explain.

Mix-Pair-Share

---

10 *World War II*

If you were President Truman, would you have chosen to drop the atomic bomb on Hiroshima? Explain your reasoning.

Mix-Pair-Share

United States Social Studies: Engaging Cooperative Learning Activities
Kagan Publishing • 800.933.2667 • www.KaganOnline.com

203

National Symbols

Cooperative Learning Activities

National Symbols
The Statue of Liberty

Directions: Think about the prompt, and then write your own response. When done, RoundRobin share your writing with your teammates. Use the space at the bottom to record ideas your teammates share.

Prompt: Read the poem *The New Colossus* by Emma Lazarus found engraved on the pedestal of the Statue of Liberty.

"Give me your tired, your poor,
Your huddled masses yearning to breathe free,
The wretched refuse of your teeming shore,
Send these, the homeless, tempest-tossed to me:
I lift my lamp beside the golden door!"

Imagine you are an immigrant coming to America. What does this poem mean to you? Explain.

My writing: _____

_____

_____

_____

_____

_____

_____

_____

_____

Ideas Teammates Share

United States Social Studies: Engaging Cooperative Learning Activities
Kagan Publishing • 800.933.2667 • www.KaganOnline.com

National Symbols
The Statue of Liberty

Directions: Think about the prompt, and then write your own response. When done, RoundRobin share your writing with your teammates. Use the space at the bottom to record ideas your teammates share.

Prompt: The Statue of Liberty took more than 20 years to complete, from idea to final construction. What character traits did the builders, artists, sailors, and others exhibit during this process? Explain your thinking.

My writing: _____

_____

_____

_____

_____

_____

_____

_____

_____

_____

_____

Ideas Teammates Share

United States Social Studies: Engaging Cooperative Learning Activities
Kagan Publishing • 800.933.2667 • www.KaganOnline.com

207

National Symbols
The Statue of Liberty

Directions: Think about the prompt, and then write your own response. When done, RoundRobin share your writing with your teammates. Use the space at the bottom to record ideas your teammates share.

> **Prompt:** The Statue of Liberty has been a symbol of freedom for immigrants since 1886. Does the Statue of Liberty still symbolize freedom today? How might it have changed? Explain your thinking.

My writing: _____

_____

_____

_____

_____

_____

_____

_____

_____

_____

_____

Ideas Teammates Share

United States Social Studies: Engaging Cooperative Learning Activities
Kagan Publishing • 800.933.2667 • www.KaganOnline.com

National Symbols

The Pledge of Allegiance

Directions: Think about the prompt, and then write your own response. When done, RoundRobin share your writing with your teammates. Use the space at the bottom to record ideas your teammates share.

Prompt: "I pledge allegiance to the flag
of the United States of America,
and to the republic
for which it stands,
one nation under God
indivisible, with liberty and justice for all."

The Pledge of Allegiance is often said in schools. Should school students be expected to say the Pledge of Allegiance during the school day? Should Americans be expected to say the Pledge of Allegiance at sporting events? Explain your thinking.

My writing: _____

_____

_____

_____

_____

_____

_____

_____

Ideas Teammates Share

United States Social Studies: Engaging Cooperative Learning Activities
Kagan Publishing • 800.933.2667 • www.KaganOnline.com

209

National Symbols
The Pledge of Allegiance

Directions: Think about the prompt, and then write your own response. When done, RoundRobin share your writing with your teammates. Use the space at the bottom to record ideas your teammates share.

Prompt: Describe what it means to pledge allegiance to the flag.

My writing: _____

_____

_____

_____

_____

_____

_____

_____

_____

Ideas Teammates Share

United States Social Studies: Engaging Cooperative Learning Activities
Kagan Publishing • 800.933.2667 • www.KaganOnline.com

National Symbols
Ellis Island / Island of Hope

Directions: Think about the prompt, and then write your own response. When done, RoundRobin share your writing with your teammates. Use the space at the bottom to record ideas your teammates share.

Prompt: Imagine yourself as a child immigrant coming to America. You are on the ship when cheers and shouts erupt signaling that Ellis Island, also known as the Island of Hope, has been spotted in the distance. Describe your feelings at seeing the Island of Hope.

My writing: _____

_____

_____

_____

_____

_____

_____

_____

_____

Ideas Teammates Share

United States Social Studies: Engaging Cooperative Learning Activities
Kagan Publishing • 800.933.2667 • www.KaganOnline.com

211

National Symbols

Ellis Island / The Journey of an Immigrant

Directions: Think about the prompt, and then write your own response. When done, RoundRobin share your writing with your teammates. Use the space at the bottom to record ideas your teammates share.

Prompt: Once immigrants arrived on Ellis Island, they were processed before being allowed into the country. Pretend you are an immigrant. Describe your journey on Ellis Island.

My writing: _____

_____

_____

_____

_____

_____

_____

_____

_____

_____

Ideas Teammates Share

United States Social Studies: Engaging Cooperative Learning Activities
Kagan Publishing • 800.933.2667 • www.KaganOnline.com

National Symbols
Ellis Island / Arriving at the Island

■ **RallyCoach Directions:** Take turns answering each question as your partner coaches. Explain your thinking to your coach.
■ **Sage-N-Scribe Directions:** The Sage describes what he or she knows about the question so the Scribe can answer the question. The Sage and Scribe switch roles for each question.

Name _____

1. Where is Ellis Island located?
   _____
   _____
   _____

2. Why were doctors on Ellis Island always observing immigrants, such as walking up the stairs?
   _____
   _____
   _____

3. What is a buttonhook?
   _____
   _____
   _____

4. What reason would an inspector use chalk to mark an immigrant's clothing?
   _____
   _____
   _____

5. Approximately how long was an immigrant's boat ride from Europe to Ellis Island?
   _____
   _____
   _____

Name _____

1. What year did Ellis Island officially open?
   _____
   _____
   _____

2. What was the first thing passengers saw when they entered New York Harbor?
   _____
   _____
   _____

3. Approximately what percentage of immigrants were sent back to their home countries?
   _____
   _____
   _____

4. Since immigrants spoke many different languages, how were they able to communicate with inspectors?
   _____
   _____
   _____

5. What is one reason an immigrant had for coming to America?
   _____
   _____
   _____

United States Social Studies: Engaging Cooperative Learning Activities
Kagan Publishing • 800.933.2667 • www.KaganOnline.com

213

National Symbols
The Pledge of Allegiance

■ **RallyCoach Directions:** Take turns answering each question as your partner coaches. Explain your thinking to your coach.
■ **Sage-N-Scribe Directions:** The Sage describes what he or she knows about the question so the Scribe can answer the question. The Sage and Scribe switch roles for each question.

"I pledge allegiance to the flag
of the United States of America,
and to the republic
for which it stands,
one nation under God
indivisible, with liberty and justice for all."

Name _____

1. What does the line, "I pledge allegiance" mean?
_____
_____
_____
_____

2. What does the line, "and to the republic" mean?
_____
_____
_____
_____

3. What does the line, "one nation under God" mean?
_____
_____
_____
_____

Name _____

1. What does the line, "of the United States of America" mean?
_____
_____
_____
_____
_____

2. What does the line, "for which it stands" mean?
_____
_____
_____
_____

3. What does the line, "indivisible, with liberty and justice for all" mean?
_____
_____
_____
_____

United States Social Studies: Engaging Cooperative Learning Activities
Kagan Publishing • 800.933.2667 • www.KaganOnline.com

National Symbols
The Pledge of Allegiance

Directions: Copy one set of cards for each team. Cut out each card along the dotted lines. Give each team a set of cards to play Fan-N-Pick or Showdown.

---

1 *National Symbols*

What does the Pledge of Allegiance symbolize?

Fan-N-Pick/Showdown

---

2 *National Symbols*

Is it a requirement by law for Americans to participate in the Pledge of Allegiance?

Fan-N-Pick/Showdown

---

3 *National Symbols*

Who wrote the Pledge of Allegiance?

Fan-N-Pick/Showdown

---

4 *National Symbols*

Where was the Pledge of Allegiance first published?

Fan-N-Pick/Showdown

---

5 *National Symbols*

Francis Bellamy wrote the pledge for students to say on _____ _____ in 1892.

Fan-N-Pick/Showdown

---

6 *National Symbols*

In 1942, Congress added the pledge to the _____ _____ _____.

Fan-N-Pick/Showdown

---

7 *National Symbols*

In 1923, the words "my flag" were changed to what phrase?

Fan-N-Pick/Showdown

---

8 *National Symbols*

What are three things people do as a sign of respect when saying the Pledge of Allegiance?

Fan-N-Pick/Showdown

---

9 *National Symbols*

What does the word "indivisible" mean?

Fan-N-Pick/Showdown

---

10 *National Symbols*

What is a symbol?

Fan-N-Pick/Showdown

United States Social Studies: Engaging Cooperative Learning Activities
Kagan Publishing • 800.933.2667 • www.KaganOnline.com

215

National Symbols
The U.S. Constitution

Directions: Copy one set of cards for each team. Cut out each card along the dotted lines. Give each team a set of cards to play Fan-N-Pick or Showdown.

1 *National Symbols* What war did the United States win in order to need its own set of rules? *Fan-N-Pick/Showdown*	**2** *National Symbols* What is the Constitutional Convention? *Fan-N-Pick/Showdown*
3 *National Symbols* What did the Founding Fathers do to help keep the meetings private? *Fan-N-Pick/Showdown*	**4** *National Symbols* Who was in charge of the Founding Fathers? *Fan-N-Pick/Showdown*
5 *National Symbols* What did some people fear would be a problem if the government was too big? *Fan-N-Pick/Showdown*	**6** *National Symbols* Which part of Congress allowed states an equal number of members? *Fan-N-Pick/Showdown*
7 *National Symbols* What is the purpose of the Bill of Rights? *Fan-N-Pick/Showdown*	**8** *National Symbols* When did the last state agree to the U.S. Constitution? *Fan-N-Pick/Showdown*
9 *National Symbols* When was the Bill of Rights added to the U.S. Constitution? *Fan-N-Pick/Showdown*	**10** *National Symbols* Which state was the first to agree to the U.S. Constitution? *Fan-N-Pick/Showdown*

216

United States Social Studies: Engaging Cooperative Learning Activities
Kagan Publishing • 800.933.2667 • www.KaganOnline.com

National Symbols
The American Flag

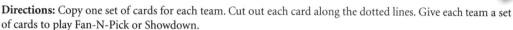

Directions: Copy one set of cards for each team. Cut out each card along the dotted lines. Give each team a set of cards to play Fan-N-Pick or Showdown.

1 *National Symbols* ★ How many stars are currently on the American flag? *Fan-N-Pick/Showdown*	**2** *National Symbols* ★ How many stripes are currently on the American flag? *Fan-N-Pick/Showdown*
3 *National Symbols* ★ Where can you see the American flag displayed? Name at least two places. *Fan-N-Pick/Showdown*	**4** *National Symbols* ★ What war, beginning in 1775, were the colonies fighting for freedom against England? *Fan-N-Pick/Showdown*
5 *National Symbols* ★ One early version of the American flag showed a rattlesnake. What did the rattlesnake warn or mean? *Fan-N-Pick/Showdown*	**6** *National Symbols* ★ What do the red and white stripes on the American flag represent? *Fan-N-Pick/Showdown*
7 *National Symbols* ★ What did Francis Scott Key do after seeing an American flag still flying after a ship attack at Fort McHenry? *Fan-N-Pick/Showdown*	**8** *National Symbols* ★ What do the stars on the American flag represent? *Fan-N-Pick/Showdown*
9 *National Symbols* ★ What caused more people to display and wear more flags after September 11, 2001? *Fan-N-Pick/Showdown*	**10** *National Symbols* ★ Which president decided the stars on the American flag would always be displayed in rows? *Fan-N-Pick/Showdown*

United States Social Studies: Engaging Cooperative Learning Activities
Kagan Publishing • 800.933.2667 • www.KaganOnline.com

217

National Symbols
The Statue of Liberty

Directions: Cut out each card along the dotted lines. Then fold each card in half so the question is on one side and the answer is on the back. Glue or tape the cards together to keep the answers and questions on opposite sides.

---

1 *National Symbols*

Why did Edouard de Laboulaye want to give a statue to the people of America?

Quiz-Quiz-Trade • Question

---

1 *National Symbols*

Why did Edouard De Laboulaye want to give a statue to the people of America?

The United States would be celebrating its 100th birthday

Quiz-Quiz-Trade • Answer

---

2 *National Symbols*

What did Frédéric Bartholdi, while designing the statue, intend for it to represent?

Quiz-Quiz-Trade • Question

---

2 *National Symbols*

What did Frédéric Bartholdi, while designing the statue, intend for it to represent?

Freedom

Quiz-Quiz-Trade • Answer

---

3 *National Symbols*

What are at least two reasons copper was used to make the statue?

Quiz-Quiz-Trade • Question

---

3 *National Symbols*

What are at least 2 reasons copper was used to make the statue?

Copper can be beaten into shape more easily than other metals, copper will not crack, copper will not rust, copper develops a protective greenish patina, the statue would be too big to be made from stone or solid metal.

Quiz-Quiz-Trade • Answer

---

4 *National Symbols*

How was the money raised to pay for the statue? Name at least two ways.

Quiz-Quiz-Trade • Question

---

4 *National Symbols*

How was the money raised to pay for the statue? Name at least two ways.

The Franco-American union, people of France, French business people, souvenirs (any two)

Quiz-Quiz-Trade • Answer

218

United States Social Studies: Engaging Cooperative Learning Activities
Kagan Publishing • 800.933.2667 • www.KaganOnline.com

National Symbols
The Statue of Liberty

Directions: Cut out each card along the dotted lines. Then fold each card in half so the question is on one side and the answer is on the back. Glue or tape the cards together to keep the answers and questions on opposite sides.

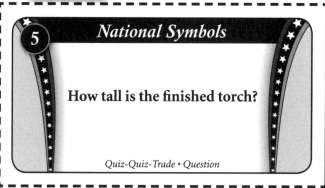

5 — *National Symbols*

How tall is the finished torch?

Quiz-Quiz-Trade • Question

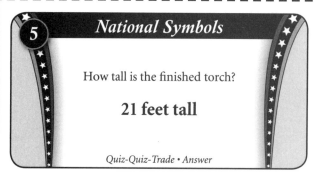

5 — *National Symbols*

How tall is the finished torch?

21 feet tall

Quiz-Quiz-Trade • Answer

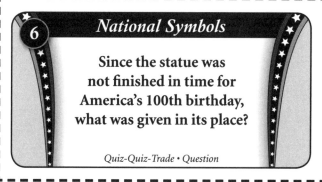

6 — *National Symbols*

Since the statue was not finished in time for America's 100th birthday, what was given in its place?

Quiz-Quiz-Trade • Question

6 — *National Symbols*

Since the statue was not finished in time for America's 100th birthday, what was given in its place?

The right hand

Quiz-Quiz-Trade • Answer

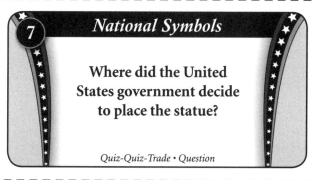

7 — *National Symbols*

Where did the United States government decide to place the statue?

Quiz-Quiz-Trade • Question

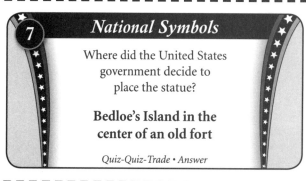

7 — *National Symbols*

Where did the United States government decide to place the statue?

Bedloe's Island in the center of an old fort

Quiz-Quiz-Trade • Answer

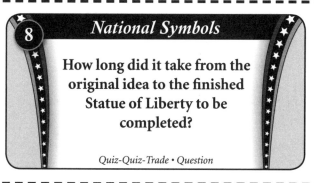

8 — *National Symbols*

How long did it take from the original idea to the finished Statue of Liberty to be completed?

Quiz-Quiz-Trade • Question

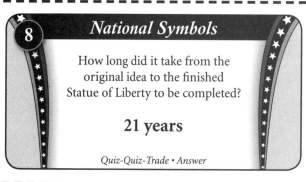

8 — *National Symbols*

How long did it take from the original idea to the finished Statue of Liberty to be completed?

21 years

Quiz-Quiz-Trade • Answer

United States Social Studies: Engaging Cooperative Learning Activities
Kagan Publishing • 800.933.2667 • www.KaganOnline.com

219

National Symbols
The Statue of Liberty

Directions: Cut out each card along the dotted lines. Then fold each card in half so the question is on one side and the answer is on the back. Glue or tape the cards together to keep the answers and questions on opposite sides.

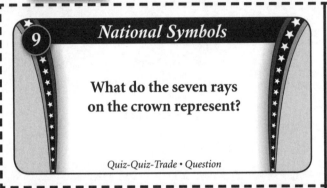

9 — *National Symbols*

What do the seven rays on the crown represent?

Quiz-Quiz-Trade • Question

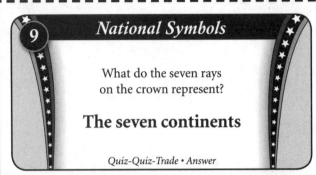

9 — *National Symbols*

What do the seven rays on the crown represent?

The seven continents

Quiz-Quiz-Trade • Answer

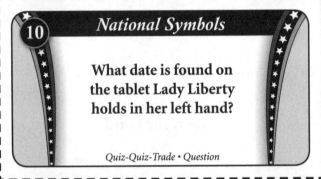

10 — *National Symbols*

What date is found on the tablet Lady Liberty holds in her left hand?

Quiz-Quiz-Trade • Question

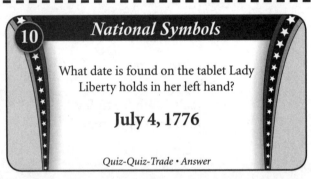

10 — *National Symbols*

What date is found on the tablet Lady Liberty holds in her left hand?

July 4, 1776

Quiz-Quiz-Trade • Answer

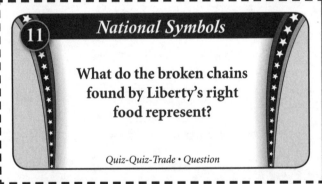

11 — *National Symbols*

What do the broken chains found by Liberty's right food represent?

Quiz-Quiz-Trade • Question

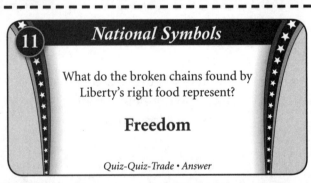

11 — *National Symbols*

What do the broken chains found by Liberty's right food represent?

Freedom

Quiz-Quiz-Trade • Answer

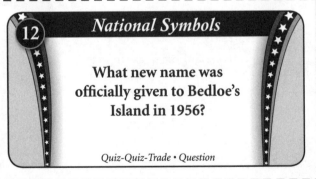

12 — *National Symbols*

What new name was officially given to Bedloe's Island in 1956?

Quiz-Quiz-Trade • Question

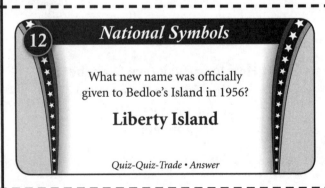

12 — *National Symbols*

What new name was officially given to Bedloe's Island in 1956?

Liberty Island

Quiz-Quiz-Trade • Answer

United States Social Studies: Engaging Cooperative Learning Activities
Kagan Publishing • 800.933.2667 • www.KaganOnline.com

National Symbols
The Statue of Liberty

Directions: Cut out each card along the dotted lines. Then fold each card in half so the question is on one side and the answer is on the back. Glue or tape the cards together to keep the answers and questions on opposite sides.

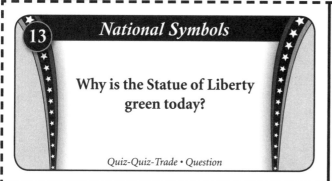

13 — *National Symbols*

Why is the Statue of Liberty green today?

Quiz-Quiz-Trade • Question

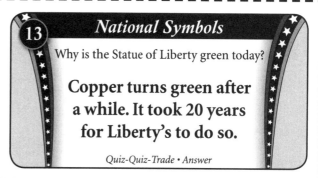

13 — *National Symbols*

Why is the Statue of Liberty green today?

Copper turns green after a while. It took 20 years for Liberty's to do so.

Quiz-Quiz-Trade • Answer

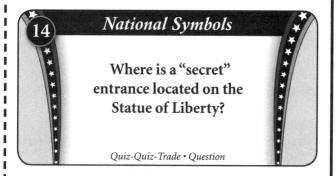

14 — *National Symbols*

Where is a "secret" entrance located on the Statue of Liberty?

Quiz-Quiz-Trade • Question

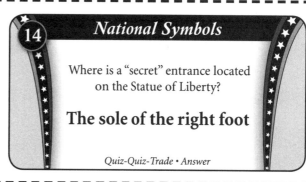

14 — *National Symbols*

Where is a "secret" entrance located on the Statue of Liberty?

The sole of the right foot

Quiz-Quiz-Trade • Answer

15 — *National Symbols*

Quiz-Quiz-Trade • Question

15 — *National Symbols*

Quiz-Quiz-Trade • Answer

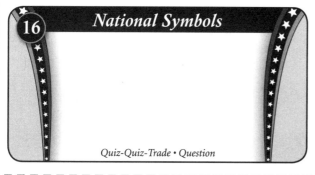

16 — *National Symbols*

Quiz-Quiz-Trade • Question

16 — *National Symbols*

Quiz-Quiz-Trade • Answer

United States Social Studies: Engaging Cooperative Learning Activities
Kagan Publishing • 800.933.2667 • www.KaganOnline.com

221

National Symbols
Historic Significance

Directions: Cut out each card along the dotted lines. Then fold each card in half so the question is on one side and the answer is on the back. Glue or tape the cards together to keep the answers and questions on opposite sides.

① National Symbols

When did the Pilgrims land in what is now Plymouth, Massachusetts?
- a) 1775
- b) 1620
- c) 1920
- d) 1834

Quiz-Quiz-Trade Question

① National Symbols

When did the Pilgrims land in what is now Plymouth, Massachusetts?

b) 1620

Quiz-Quiz-Trade Answer

② National Symbols

Where was the nation's capital located before it was moved to Washington, D.C. in 1800?
- a) Springfield, Illinois
- b) Liberty, Missouri
- c) New York, New York
- d) Philadelphia, Pennsylvania

Quiz-Quiz-Trade Question

② National Symbols

Where was the nation's capital located before it was moved to Washington, D.C. in 1800?

d) Philadelphia, Pennsylvania

Quiz-Quiz-Trade Answer

③ National Symbols

Who is the only president NOT to live in the White House?
- a) James Madison
- b) William Taft
- c) George Washington
- d) Abraham Lincoln

Quiz-Quiz-Trade Question

③ National Symbols

Who is the only president NOT to live in the White House?

c) George Washington

Quiz-Quiz-Trade Answer

④ National Symbols

What words are found carved in the front of the Supreme Court Building?
- a) Equal Justice Under Law
- b) All Is Fair and Just
- c) Life, Liberty, and the Pursuit of Happiness
- d) One Nation Under God

Quiz-Quiz-Trade Question

④ National Symbols

What words are found carved in the front of the Supreme Court Building?

a) Equal Justice Under Law

Quiz-Quiz-Trade Answer

United States Social Studies: Engaging Cooperative Learning Activities
Kagan Publishing • 800.933.2667 • www.KaganOnline.com

National Symbols
Historic Significance

Directions: Cut out each card along the dotted lines. Then fold each card in half so the question is on one side and the answer is on the back. Glue or tape the cards together to keep the answers and questions on opposite sides.

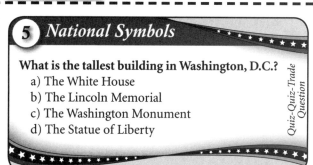

5 National Symbols

What is the tallest building in Washington, D.C.?
a) The White House
b) The Lincoln Memorial
c) The Washington Monument
d) The Statue of Liberty

Quiz-Quiz-Trade Question

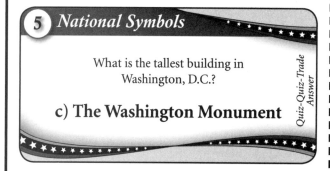

5 National Symbols

What is the tallest building in Washington, D.C.?

c) The Washington Monument

Quiz-Quiz-Trade Answer

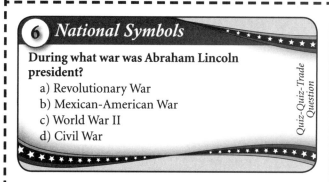

6 National Symbols

During what war was Abraham Lincoln president?
a) Revolutionary War
b) Mexican-American War
c) World War II
d) Civil War

Quiz-Quiz-Trade Question

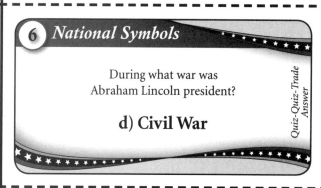

6 National Symbols

During what war was Abraham Lincoln president?

d) Civil War

Quiz-Quiz-Trade Answer

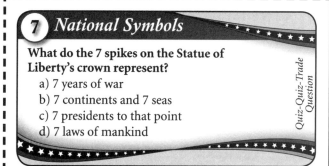

7 National Symbols

What do the 7 spikes on the Statue of Liberty's crown represent?
a) 7 years of war
b) 7 continents and 7 seas
c) 7 presidents to that point
d) 7 laws of mankind

Quiz-Quiz-Trade Question

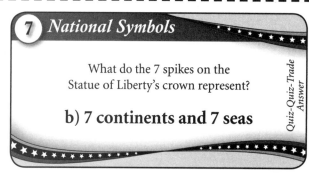

7 National Symbols

What do the 7 spikes on the Statue of Liberty's crown represent?

b) 7 continents and 7 seas

Quiz-Quiz-Trade Answer

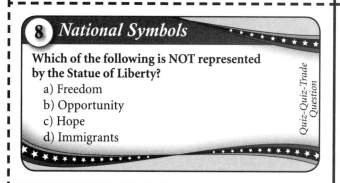

8 National Symbols

Which of the following is NOT represented by the Statue of Liberty?
a) Freedom
b) Opportunity
c) Hope
d) Immigrants

Quiz-Quiz-Trade Question

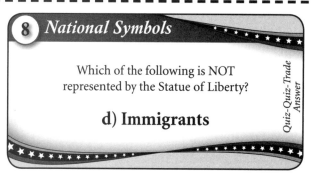

8 National Symbols

Which of the following is NOT represented by the Statue of Liberty?

d) Immigrants

Quiz-Quiz-Trade Answer

United States Social Studies: Engaging Cooperative Learning Activities
Kagan Publishing • 800.933.2667 • www.KaganOnline.com

223

National Symbols
Historic Significance

Directions: Cut out each card along the dotted lines. Then fold each card in half so the question is on one side and the answer is on the back. Glue or tape the cards together to keep the answers and questions on opposite sides.

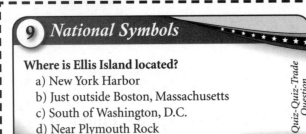

9 National Symbols

Where is Ellis Island located?
- a) New York Harbor
- b) Just outside Boston, Massachusetts
- c) South of Washington, D.C.
- d) Near Plymouth Rock

Quiz-Quiz-Trade Question

9 National Symbols

Where is Ellis Island located?

a) New York Harbor

Quiz-Quiz-Trade Answer

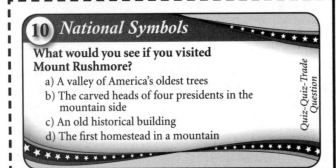

10 National Symbols

What would you see if you visited Mount Rushmore?
- a) A valley of America's oldest trees
- b) The carved heads of four presidents in the mountain side
- c) An old historical building
- d) The first homestead in a mountain

Quiz-Quiz-Trade Question

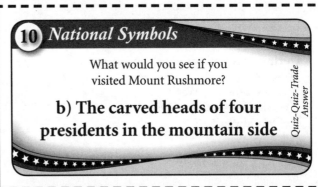

10 National Symbols

What would you see if you visited Mount Rushmore?

b) The carved heads of four presidents in the mountain side

Quiz-Quiz-Trade Answer

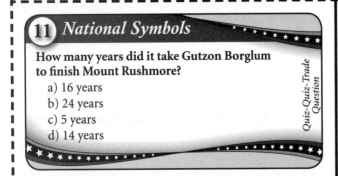

11 National Symbols

How many years did it take Gutzon Borglum to finish Mount Rushmore?
- a) 16 years
- b) 24 years
- c) 5 years
- d) 14 years

Quiz-Quiz-Trade Question

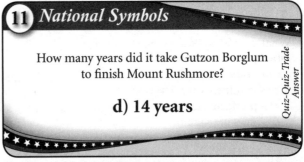

11 National Symbols

How many years did it take Gutzon Borglum to finish Mount Rushmore?

d) 14 years

Quiz-Quiz-Trade Answer

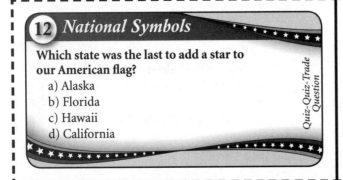

12 National Symbols

Which state was the last to add a star to our American flag?
- a) Alaska
- b) Florida
- c) Hawaii
- d) California

Quiz-Quiz-Trade Question

12 National Symbols

Which state was the last to add a star to our American flag?

c) Hawaii

Quiz-Quiz-Trade Answer

United States Social Studies: Engaging Cooperative Learning Activities
Kagan Publishing • 800.933.2667 • www.KaganOnline.com

National Symbols
Historic Significance

Directions: Cut out each card along the dotted lines. Then fold each card in half so the question is on one side and the answer is on the back. Glue or tape the cards together to keep the answers and questions on opposite sides.

13 National Symbols

Why was the Liberty Bell rung on July 8, 1776?
- a) To warn of possible intruders
- b) To celebrate the first reading of the Declaration of Independence
- c) Announce the ending of the war
- d) Welcome the new President of the United States

Quiz-Quiz-Trade Question

13 National Symbols

Why was the liberty bell rang on July 8th, 1776?

b) To celebrate the first reading of the Declaration of Independence

Quiz-Quiz-Trade Answer

14 National Symbols

What bird did Benjamin Franklin want as our national bird?
- a) Wild turkey
- b) Bald eagle
- c) Golden falcon
- d) Red robin

Quiz-Quiz-Trade Question

14 National Symbols

What bird did Benjamin Franklin want as our national bird?

a) Wild turkey

Quiz-Quiz-Trade Answer

15 National Symbols

What does the number 13, found in stars, stripes, and arrows, represent on the Great Seal?
- a) The number of founding fathers
- b) The original 13 Colonies
- c) The years America fought in wars
- d) The number of laws in the Constitution

Quiz-Quiz-Trade Question

15 National Symbols

What does the number 13, found in stars, stripes, and arrows, represent?

b) The original 13 Colonies

Quiz-Quiz-Trade Answer

16 National Symbols

What was the purpose of the Declaration of Independence?
- a) Persuade Great Britain to free the colonies
- b) Ask for more supplies to help the starving colonists
- c) List the unfair things Great Britain had done, and declare the colonies free
- d) Appoint the new president

Quiz-Quiz-Trade Question

16 National Symbols

What was the purpose of the Declaration of Independence?

c) List the unfair things Great Britain had done, and declare the colonies free

Quiz-Quiz-Trade Answer

United States Social Studies: Engaging Cooperative Learning Activities
Kagan Publishing • 800.933.2667 • www.KaganOnline.com

225

National Symbols
Historic Significance

Directions: Cut out each card along the dotted lines. Then fold each card in half so the question is on one side and the answer is on the back. Glue or tape the cards together to keep the answers and questions on opposite sides.

(17) National Symbols

What is a constitution?
a) A formal school for presidents
b) A building for secret government meetings
c) The formal declaration of war
d) The written ideas and rules that show how a country will be run

Quiz-Quiz-Trade Question

(17) National Symbols

What is a constitution?

d) The written ideas and rules that show how a country will be run

Quiz-Quiz-Trade Answer

(18) National Symbols

What accomplishment did Francis Scott Key perform?
a) Wrote the National Anthem
b) Delivered the news that Fort McHenry had fallen
c) Created the Great Seal
d) Drafted the first Pledge of Allegiance

Quiz-Quiz-Trade Question

(18) National Symbols

What accomplishment did Francis Scott Key perform?

a) Wrote the National Anthem

Quiz-Quiz-Trade Answer

(19) National Symbols

What does "allegiance" mean?
a) To promise to be loyal and true
b) To follow without question
c) To be a part of something greater
d) To be a friend

Quiz-Quiz-Trade Question

(19) National Symbols

What does "allegiance" mean?

a) To promise to be loyal and true

Quiz-Quiz-Trade Answer

(20) National Symbols

What is honored on Memorial Day?
a) The end of the school year
b) Time with family and friends
c) Americans who died in all wars
d) The end of the Revolutionary War

Quiz-Quiz-Trade Question

(20) National Symbols

What is honored on Memorial Day?

c) Americans who died in all wars

Quiz-Quiz-Trade Answer

United States Social Studies: Engaging Cooperative Learning Activities
Kagan Publishing • 800.933.2667 • www.KaganOnline.com

National Symbols
Historic Significance

Directions: Cut out each card along the dotted lines. Then fold each card in half so the question is on one side and the answer is on the back. Glue or tape the cards together to keep the answers and questions on opposite sides.

21 *National Symbols*

Which holiday requires all government buildings to fly the American flag?
  a) Labor Day
  b) Thanksgiving
  c) Christmas
  d) Flag Day

Quiz-Quiz-Trade Question

21 *National Symbols*

Which holiday requires all government buildings to fly the American flag?

d) Flag Day

Quiz-Quiz-Trade Answer

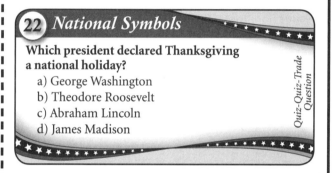

22 *National Symbols*

Which president declared Thanksgiving a national holiday?
  a) George Washington
  b) Theodore Roosevelt
  c) Abraham Lincoln
  d) James Madison

Quiz-Quiz-Trade Question

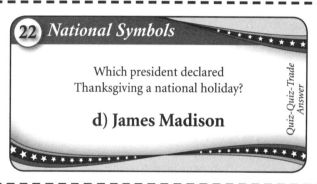

22 *National Symbols*

Which president declared Thanksgiving a national holiday?

d) James Madison

Quiz-Quiz-Trade Answer

23 *National Symbols*

Quiz-Quiz-Trade Question

23 *National Symbols*

Quiz-Quiz-Trade Answer

24 *National Symbols*

Quiz-Quiz-Trade Question

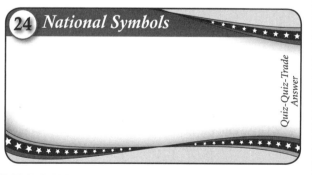

24 *National Symbols*

Quiz-Quiz-Trade Answer

United States Social Studies: Engaging Cooperative Learning Activities
Kagan Publishing • 800.933.2667 • www.KaganOnline.com

227

National Symbols
Ellis Island / The Life of an Immigrant

Directions: The class "mixes" until the teacher calls, "pair." Students find a new partner to discuss or answer the teacher's question.

1 *National Symbols*

Imagine you are a child immigrant and coming to Ellis Island.

Describe your thoughts during the 2 week boat ride to America.

Mix-Pair-Share

2 *National Symbols*

Immigrants were often told that the streets of America were paved with gold.

What does the phrase "paved with gold" mean to immigrants?

Mix-Pair-Share

3 *National Symbols*

Immigrants came to America for different reasons.

Pretend you are an immigrant and have left your home country. Describe your reasons for wanting to travel to America.

Mix-Pair-Share

4 *National Symbols*

Inspectors were everywhere on Ellis Island watching immigrants.

Imagine you were an inspector. Describe what you are observing as you watch immigrants arrive.

Mix-Pair-Share

5 *National Symbols*

You are an immigrant that has just had the medical exam. The inspector used chalk to mark on your clothing.

Describe your feelings and thoughts at this discovery.

Mix-Pair-Share

6 *National Symbols*

Immigrant children often made the journey to America alone, sometimes to rejoin with parents.

What possible thoughts or worries might an immigrant child have upon rejoining family in a new country?

Mix-Pair-Share

7 *National Symbols*

You are an immigrant that has just been ferried to Ellis Island. Describe your journey through Ellis Island before being allowed into America.

Mix-Pair-Share

8 *National Symbols*

Approximately 2% of immigrants were forced to return to their home country. Describe the heartache that news may cause.

Mix-Pair-Share

9 *National Symbols*

After being processed through Ellis Island, immigrants entered America. What would the next part of the journey be for an immigrant? Use your imagination.

Mix-Pair-Share

10 *National Symbols*

You have been asked to learn more about Ellis Island and immigration. What steps would you take to learn more information?

Mix-Pair-Share

228

United States Social Studies: Engaging Cooperative Learning Activities
Kagan Publishing • 800.933.2667 • www.KaganOnline.com

U.S. *Social Studies Answer Key*

U.S. Social Studies
Answer Key

American Indians

◆ RallyCoach/Sage-N-Scribe (pp. 37–38)

Page 37

Left Column
1. a) Pawnee
2. d) Deer, bear, beaver, elk
3. a) They built canoes of birch bark.
4. d) Haudenosaunee

Right Column
1. c) Eastern Woodlands Cultural Region
2. b) Longhouse
3. b) Wampum
4. b) Tribes sent male representatives to the Great Council to make decisions for the league.

Page 38

Left Column
1. a) Inuit
2. b) Cedar trees
3. a) Help heal people who were ill
4. b) Homes were built of sturdy planks and logs from the cedar trees.

Right Column
1. c) Oregon
2. d) Totem poles
3. d) Sharks
4. b) Potlatches

◆ Fan-N-Pick/Showdown (p. 39)
1. Lakota (Sioux), Pawnee, Osage, Cheyenne
2. dry, vast lands
3. Buffalo
4. Lodge
5. Tepee
6. Horses
7. Spanish (Spain)
8. Montana
9. Corn, beans, squash, pumpkins
10. bows and arrows

◆ Find Someone Who (p. 40)
1. Apache, Navajo, Hopi, Zuni, Pueblo
2. Hot and arid, dry
3. Irrigation system
4. Own property, weave baskets
5. Weave cloth
6. Built high off ground (in stones), used adobe
7. Answers will vary
8. Texas, Arizona, New Mexico, Utah
9. To tell young Hopi Indians the tribal history

◆ Mix-N-Match (pp. 41–43)

Page 41

Tribe: Iroquois
Dwelling: Longhouse

Tribe: Cheyenne
Dwelling: Tepee

Tribe: Great Plains Indians
Dwelling: Lodge

Tribe: Hopi
Dwelling: Adobe

Page 42

Tribe: Algonquian Indians
Dwelling: Wigwam

Tribe: Southeastern Indians
Dwelling: Wattle and Daub house

Tribe: Southern Plains Indians
Dwelling: Grass house

Tribe: Seminole Indians
Dwelling: Chickees

United States Social Studies: Engaging Cooperative Learning Activities
Kagan Publishing • 800.933.2667 • www.KaganOnline.com

American Indians *(Continued)*

◆ Mix-N-Match (pp. 41–43) *(Continued)*

Page 43

Tribe: West Coast and Plateau Indians
Dwelling: Earthen house

Tribe: Northwest Coast Indians
Dwelling: Plank houses

Tribe: Inuit Indians
Dwelling: Igloo

The American Colonies

◆ RallyCoach/Sage-N-Scribe (p. 47)

Left Column

1. d) Raised crops such as barley and rye
2. a) Manufacturing of items such as leather good
3. c) Rhode Island
4. a) To give debtors from England a fresh start rather than place them in a crowded English jail

Right Column

1. b) Virginia
2. c) Southern colonies
3. a) Thomas Hooker
4. c) Offered separation between the colonies and Spanish Florida

◆ Fan-N-Pick/Showdown (pp. 48–51)

Page 48

1. Selling stock
2. Land was not great for house building, mosquitoes carried disease, undrinkable water
3. John Smith
4. Tobacco
5. Indentured servant
6. House of Burgesses
7. Northwest Passage
8. Explore, freedom of religion, fresh start, economic opportunity

Page 49

9. Person who travels to a new location for religious reasons
10. Wanted to separate from church of England, faced persecution
11. Mayflower Compact
12. Thankful to survive winter
13. Puritans
14. Puritans

Page 50

1. Answers will vary
2. Answers will vary
3. Answers will vary
4. Answers will vary
5. Answers will vary
6. Answers will vary
7. Answers will vary
8. Answers will vary

Page 51

9. Answers will vary
10. Answers will vary
11. Answers will vary
12. Answers will vary

(Continued)

United States Social Studies: Engaging Cooperative Learning Activities
Kagan Publishing • 800.933.2667 • www.KaganOnline.com

231

U.S. Social Studies
Answer Key

The American Colonies (Continued)

◆ Mix-N-Match (pp. 52–54)

Page 52

John White: Led more than 100 people to Roanoake Island but returned to England for supplies, upon his return discovered the colony had disappeared

Walter Raleigh: Adviser to Queen Elizabeth, agreed to organize the first colony of Roanoake, solider familiar with North America

Roanoke Island: England's first attempt at creating an American Colony, faced difficult times and starvation caused many to return to England. A second attempt in 1587 proved hard and by August 1590, the colony had mysteriously disappeared

Jamestown Colony: Group of merchants formed this colony in 1606, founded in Virginia

Page 53

Charter: Document which allowed colonist to settle on new land that was claimed by the ruler of his or her home country

John Smith: Elected leader of Jamestown Colony, traded with leader of the Powhatan Indian people, life saved by Pocahontas

Pocahontas: Young daughter of Chief Powhtatan, leader of Powhtatan people, at age 12 saved life of John Smith

Indentured Servant: Someone who agrees to work for a set number of years in exchange for the cost of journeying overseas to North America

Page 54

House of Burgesses: First law making assembly in an English Colony

New England Colonies: Group of colonies know for the first emigrants including Puritan separatists later known as Pilgrims, Massachusetts Bay Company sent large group to establish Massachusetts settlement, also included colonies of Connecticut, Rhode Island and New Hampshire

The Middle Colonies: Group of colonies known for being occupied by Dutch traders and landowners, area became known as New York, land west of Delaware was given to Quaker William Penn and developed colony eventually known as Pennsylvania

Southern Colonies: Group of colonies that began south of Virginia and stretched down to Florida, known for farming and plantations which produced varying crops, relied on African slave labor from Barbados

The American Revolution

◆ RallyCoach/Sage-N-Scribe (pp. 59–60)

Page 59

Left Column

1. b) Tea could only be purchased through the East India Tea Company.
2. a) Patriots
3. a) An unknown shot was fired.
4. c) The minutemen stayed up all night to prepare the fort and then eventually ran out of ammunition.

Right Column

1. c) Britain imposed higher taxes and stricter penalties.
2. b) Loyalists
3. b) The women hid all the minutemen's weapons in fields and barns over town so the British wouldn't discover them.
4. b) *"Don't fire till you see the whites of their eyes."*

United States Social Studies: Engaging Cooperative Learning Activities
Kagan Publishing • 800.933.2667 • www.KaganOnline.com

The American Revolution *(Continued)*

◆ RallyCoach/Sage-N-Scribe (pp. 59–60) *(Continued)*

Page 60

Left Column
1. b) America was fighting for independence.
2. d) Everyone was well fed.
3. c) The words written by Thomas Paine
4. c) Battle of Trenton
5. c) Slow the enemy down

Right Column
1. d) George Washington
2. a) German soldier fighting for the British
3. a) The water was frozen in places and chunks of ice had to be removed.
4. b) Appealed to the love of the country
5. a) Courageous

◆ Find Someone Who (pp. 67–69)

Page 67

1. b) The French and Indian War was very costly.
2. a) A tax on printed materials in the colonies
3. d) Patrick Henry
4. a) The Townshend Act took its place.
5. d) Britain raised taxes in their homeland.
6. d) Sons of Liberty
7. b) The Boston Massacre
8. b) A tariff or tax on imported goods
9. a) Committee of Correspondence

Page 68

1. George Washington
2. Continental Army
3. John Hancock
4. Olive Branch Petition
5. Thomas Paine
6. Thomas Jefferson
7. July 4, 1776
8. Hessians
9. Battle of Saratoga

Page 69

1. Boston Tea Party
2. The shot heard round the world
3. Second Continental Congress
4. Washington takes command of Continental Army
5. Washington's troops won second battle of Trenton
6. King Louis XVI of France signed treaty
7. England signed peace treaty declaring total independence
8. Washington chosen president of Constitutional Convention
9. Stamp Act goes into effect

◆ Mix-N-Match (pp. 70–72)

Page 70

Cause: French and Indian War
Effect: Parliament passed the Stamp Act

Cause: The Stamp Act
Effect: Sons of Liberty formed

Cause: Parliament repealed the Stamp Act
Effect: Parliament passed the Townshend Act

Cause: Parliament passed the Townshend Act
Effect: Colonist boycotted British goods

Page 71

Cause: Rising tension in Boston in 1776
Effect: Boston Massacre

Cause: Colonial boycotts hurt British businesses
Effect: Britain cancels all taxes except the Tea Tax

Cause: Parliament passes the Tea Act
Effect: Boston Tea Party

Cause: Boston Tea Party
Effect: The Intolerable Acts

(Continued)

United States Social Studies: Engaging Cooperative Learning Activities
Kagan Publishing • 800.933.2667 • www.KaganOnline.com

233

U.S. Social Studies
Answer Key

The American Revolution *(Continued)*

◆ Mix-N-Match (pp. 70–72) *(Continued)*

Page 72

Cause: The Intolerable Acts
Effect: Colonists took sides as Patriots or Loyalists

Cause: First Continental Congress
Effect: Colonist began training militia

Cause: On April 19, 1775, an unknown shot was fired in Lexington, Virginia.
Effect: British soldiers opened fire on the Minutemen and war broke out. This became known as "the shot heard around the world."

Cause: King George refused to read *The Olive Branch Petition*
Effect: The Second Continental Congress wrote *The Declaration of Independence*

Historic Documents

◆ RallyCoach/Sage-N-Scribe (pp. 84–85)

Page 84

Left Column
1. b) To outline the plan for the new national government
2. d) Created a central government
3. c) Shay's Rebellion and raids in Massachusetts
4. c) There was no president or monarch in power

Right Column
1. a) All thirteen states had to ratify or approve it
2. c) Nine states
3. b) Create and collect taxes
4. b) 8 years

Page 85

Left Column
1. a) 1783
2. d) A special meeting in Philadelphia
3. b) James Madison
4. a) The air conditioner was broken.
5. c) To explain how the government works

Right Column
1. b) Thirteen
2. a) Founding Fathers
3. c) Small states should have as many votes as large states.
4. b) We the people,
5. b) September 17, 1787

◆ Fan-N-Pick/Showdown (p. 86)

1. Revolutionary War
2. Special meeting in Philadelphia to plan a better government
3. Closed the windows, locked the doors, and posted guards
4. George Washington
5. States would lose too much power
6. Senate
7. to explain the freedoms of the people
8. June 21, 1788
9. 1791
10. Delaware

◆ Find Someone Who (p. 87)

1. c) Thomas Jefferson
2. a) James Monroe
3. b) July 4, 1776
4. a) John Hancock
5. d) Committee of Five
6. c) 56
7. b) Thomas Jefferson and John Adams
8. c) He hoped for a reconciliation with Britain.
9. d) National Archives Building in Washington, D.C.

234

United States Social Studies: Engaging Cooperative Learning Activities
Kagan Publishing • 800.933.2667 • www.KaganOnline.com

Historic Documents (Continued)

◆ Mix-N-Match (pp. 88–90)

Page 88
First: Freedom of speech, religion, press, assemble peacefully, voice complaints against the government

Second: Own and bare firearms

Third: Government cannot force citizens to house soldiers during peacetime.

Fourth: Unfair search and seizures of property

Page 89
Fifth: No one can be deprived of life, liberty, and the pursuit of happiness without the decision of the court of law.

Sixth: Right to trial by jury and a lawyer in criminal cases

Seventh: Right to trial by jury in most civil cases

Eighth: Prohibits high bail bonds, extreme punishments, and very high fines

Page 90
Ninth: Rights of people are not limited to those stated in the Constitution.

Tenth: Powers not granted to the federal government are decided by the state government or the people.

Formation of a New Government

◆ RallyCoach/Sage-N-Scribe (pp. 100–101)

Page 100
Left Column
1. a) President
2. c) 2 years
3. d) Depends on number of people in the state
4. a) Serve in the military
5. b) 6 years

Right Column
1. a) To make our laws
2. d) The House of Representatives and Senate
3. b) 2 years
4. d) Two senators
5. d) Be born in the state they represent

Page 101
Left Column
1. d) Unlawful search and seizure
2. b) Right to a fair and speedy trial
3. b) Powers not given to the federal government in the Constitution belong to the state or to the people.
4. d) Thirteenth Amendment
5. a) First Amendment

Right Column
1. a) Fifth Amendment
2. c) Death penalty
3. a) Women are given the right to vote.
4. c) Second Amendment
5. d) Twenty-Sixth Amendment

◆ Fan-N-Pick/Showdown (p. 102)
1. U.S. citizens over the age of 18 are allowed to vote.
2. Right to bear arms
3. The Third Amendment
4. Right to a jury trial in civil suits
5. The rights cannot go against, or infringe upon, rights of the citizens that are not specifically listed in the Constitution.
6. Slavery
7. Freedom of speech, religion, press, assembly, and petition
8. The Nineteenth Amendment
9. The Fourth Amendment
10. The Twenty-Second Amendment

(Continued)

United States Social Studies: Engaging Cooperative Learning Activities
Kagan Publishing • 800.933.2667 • www.KaganOnline.com

235

U.S. Social Studies
Answer Key

Formation of a New Government (Continued)

◆ Find Someone Who (pp. 108–110)

Page 108

1. Make sure laws are obeyed
2. President
3. President of Senate; takes over presidency if current president can't serve
4. Advise president and help carry out policies
5. Determine order of succession, who becomes president order
6. 35 years old
7. Answers will vary
8. Secretary of State
9. Answers will vary

Page 109

1. Executive branch
2. Legislative branch
3. Judicial branch
4. President
5. Two-thirds majority must rule in favor
6. Judicial branch
7. Legislative branch
8. Judicial branch
9. Checks and Balances

Page 110

1. Legislative branch
2. Legislative branch
3. Francis Scott Key
4. Legislative, judicial, executive
5. Bill of Rights
6. Judicial branch
7. 50 states
8. Declaration of Independence
9. Washington, D.C.
10. Red
11. Executive branch
12. Executive branch

Westward Expansion

◆ RallyCoach/Sage-N-Scribe (pp. 116–118)

Page 116

Left Column

1. b) Saint Joseph, Missouri
2. a) To deliver mail in a shortened amount of time
3. d) Animal attacks
4. c) Overland Stage Company
5. b) October 1861

Right Column

1. d) January 1860
2. c) To be seen easily from a distance
3. b) Telegraph
4. b) Around 250
5. d) The coaches could carry magazines and packages.

Page 117

Left Column

1. a) Belief that all people should come together with pride in their country
2. d) Andrew Jackson
3. c) $5 million

Right Column

1. b) Warn European countries against interfering with America
2. a) Spain had trouble defending Florida.
3. b) Russia and Britain

Page 118

Left Column

1. a) President Thomas Jefferson
2. d) She could help trade with American Indians.
3. b) Shoshone
4. d) 15
5. c) The east was getting crowded and the territory would double America's size.

Right Column

1. c) Corps of Discovery
2. a) To update President Jefferson about the journey so far
3. b) France
4. a) More than 2 years
5. b) He could act as a translator.

United States Social Studies: Engaging Cooperative Learning Activities
Kagan Publishing • 800.933.2667 • www.KaganOnline.com

Westward Expansion (Continued)

◆ Fan-N-Pick/Showdown (pp. 119–120)

Page 119

1. Cherokee, Creek, Chickasaw, Choctaw
2. Indian Removal Act
3. Move American Indians to new Indian territory
4. Oklahoma
6. Andrew Jackson
5. Cherokee
8. Trail of tears
7. 15,000

Page 120

1. Thomas Jefferson
2. Trade routes
3. James Madison
4. France
5. Napoleon
6. 1803
7. $15 million
8. Doubled
9. He needed money for war against Britain
10. New Orleans

◆ Find Someone Who (pp. 126–127)

Page 126

1. $25 a week
2. The discovery of gold
3. Flooded rivers, mountain snows, Indian attacks, starvation, or disease (any two)
4. Kept on riding
5. Not to use profane language, get drunk, gamble, treat animals cruelly, do anything else that is not like a gentlemen (any two)
6. Ferryboat
7. Army troops and a group of California militia arrived
8. Mochila
9. One

Page 127

1. b) James Madison
2. a) The majority of war was at sea.
3. c) The U.S. wanted to take over Great Britain's sea trade routes.
4. b) It prospered because more goods were made at home.
5. c) The Federalist party
6. b) Old Ironsides
7. b) The capital city and the president's house were burned and in control of Britain.
8. b) The National Anthem
9. a) Victory at the Battle of New Orleans

The Civil War and Reconstruction

◆ RallyCoach/Sage-N-Scribe (pp. 137–139)

Page 137

Left Column
1. c) People in the north work in factories located in cities when people in the south live a rural way of life working on farms.
2. a) Tax on imported goods
3. a) Missouri

Right Column
1. c) The Continental Congress publicly announcing the end of owning slaves
2. b) Slavery is wrong and should be ended
3. b) Abraham Lincoln is elected president.

Page 138

Left Column
1. c) Both men attended the U.S. Military Academy at West Point.
2. c) He was the 18th president.
3. a) The assault on Fort Donelson
4. b) He was born in Ohio as the son of a wealthy leather tanner.

Right Column
1. c) He was the Commander of the Union Army
2. a) The Spanish-American War
3. a) Farming
4. a) His understanding of horses lead to a job of training horses.

(Continued)

United States Social Studies: Engaging Cooperative Learning Activities
Kagan Publishing • 800.933.2667 • www.KaganOnline.com

237

U.S. Social Studies
Answer Key

The Civil War and Reconstruction (Continued)

◆ RallyCoach/Sage-N-Scribe (pp. 137–139) (Continued)

Page 139

Left Column

1. c) President Lincoln was assassinated while attending a production at Ford's Theatre.
2. a) Laws that limit the rights of former slaves.
3. d) Andrew Johnson was removed from office following his impeachment.

Right Column

1. b) Abolished slavery in all states
2. c) Freedmen's Bureau
3. b) A law that enforced the segregation between white Americans and freed African Americans

◆ Find Someone Who (pp. 145–146)

Page 145

1. Varies: better military leaders, hunters familiar with weapons
4. Shutting off an area (sea, land, or air) to keep out supplies
7. Laws to control a slave's behavior

2. Varies: more weapons, railroads, canals and roads
5. Richmond, Virginia
8. Sherman's March

3. Went to other locations for cotton
6. Battle of Antietam
9. Law requiring men of certain age to join military

Page 146

1. d) Virginia
4. b) He graduated second in his class from West Point without any demerits.
7. a) President of Washington College

2. a) His father died when he was 11, and his mother instilled strong moral values.
5. c) Virginia succeeded and he did not want to fight against his home and family.
8. b) Traveler, his horse, walked behind Lee's casket.

3. b) The academy was free to men from Virginia, and he was the son of a war hero.
6. b) He considered slavery a moral and political evil and rejoiced in the abolishment of slavery.
9. b) His papers were never processed.

◆ Mix-N-Match (pp. 147–149)

Page 147

Clara Barton: Founded the Red Cross in 1881 after nursing wounded soldiers during the Civil War

Robert Shaw: Commander of the 54th Regiment, which was one of the first African-American units serving in the Civil War

Robert E. Lee: General of the Confederate Army

Ulysses S. Grant: Fourth general to lead the Union Forces, later elected president for two terms

Page 148

Harriet Tubman: Famous "conductor" of the underground railroad after escaping slavery herself

Harriet Beecher Stowe: Author of Uncle Tom's Cabin depicting the cruelty of slavery

Abraham Lincoln: Republican elected the 16th president of the United States in 1860

Stephen Douglas: Democratic senator who ran against Lincoln for president

Page 149

Jefferson Davis: Senator from Mississippi elected president for the Confederacy

Thomas "Stonewall" Jackson: General from Virginia who defeated the Union army in Virginia, fought in The First Battle of Bull Run

General Winfield Scott: Fought in the Mexican War and provided advice on war strategy to President Lincoln

Henry Clay: Known as "The Great Compromise" and proposed the Missouri Compromise

238

United States Social Studies: Engaging Cooperative Learning Activities
Kagan Publishing • 800.933.2667 • www.KaganOnline.com

Industrialization

◆ RallyCoach/Sage-N-Scribe (p. 162)

Left Column
1. b) Abraham Lincoln
2. c) News could travel fast but it still took a long time for people and goods.
3. a) Pacific Railway Act
4. a) Union Pacific

Right Column
1. b) Union Pacific and Central Pacific
2. d) Funding for the railroad ran out midway through completion.
3. c) Omaha, Nebraska
4. b) Blasting tunnels through solid rock with dynamite

◆ Fan-N-Pick/Showdown (pp. 163–164)

Page 163
1. Sinking of Maine Battleship, angered by the treatment of Cubans, newspapers dramatized issues
3. Reported sinking of Maine Battleship with no evidence Spain did it
5. Rough Riders
7. Sinking of the Maine Battleship

2. Puerto Rico, Guam, Philippines
4. President McKinley
6. Assistant Secretary of the Navy
8. Imprisoned hundreds of Cubans

Page 164
1. Seneca Falls Convention
3. Susan B. Anthony Amendment
5. Suffrage
7. Suffragists
9. Jeannette Rankin

2. Nineteenth
4. Women took over jobs typically held by men
6. True
8. National Women's Party
10. Education, ownership of property

◆ Find Someone Who (p. 165)

1. c) Men, women, and children often worked over 12 hours a day, 7 days a week in poor conditions.
4. d) A cigar factory worker who was one of the first union leaders who helped form the American Federation of Labor

2. b) A cramped, hot workshop, often where women operated sewing machines
5. c) An 8-hour work day

3. b) Employers join together in order to get the best performance from employees.
6. c) Labor Day

◆ Mix-N-Match (pp. 166–168)

Page 166

New Process for Steel Making: Bessemer developed the Bessemer process in 1885 allowing for better construction of buildings and bridges.

First Reliable Steam Engine: James Watt invented this in 1775 allowing faster transportation of goods and people.

Cotton Gin: Eli Whitney invented this in 1793 to remove cotton from its seeds.

Telegraph: Samuel F. B. Morse invented this in 1836, which allowed messages to be transmitted over a wire.

(Continued)

United States Social Studies: Engaging Cooperative Learning Activities
Kagan Publishing • 800.933.2667 • www.KaganOnline.com

239

U.S. Social Studies
Answer Key

Industrialization *(Continued)*

◆ Mix-N-Match (pp. 166–168) *(Continued)*

Page 167

Sewing Machine: Elias Howe invented this in 1844 to speed up the process of garment making.

Typewriter: Christopher Latham Sholes builds this in 1873 allowing for printed text.

Telephone: Alexander Graham Bell invented this in 1876, which allowed communication across distances.

Long Lasting Light Bulb: Thomas Edison invented this in 1879, and by 1880, these were used to light city streets.

Page 168

Electric Motor: Nikola Tesla invented this in 1888, which led to future inventions.

Radio: Italy's Gigliemo Marconi invented this in 1895, providing a fast way to receive news.

World War I

◆ RallyCoach/Sage-N-Scribe (p. 174)

Left Column
1. b) Allied Powers
2. b) Poison gas
3. d) Woodrow Wilson
4. c) Act as an international organization to prevent wars

Right Column
1. a) Central Powers
2. a) The airplanes fought in the air and dropped bombs.
3. b) Veteran's Day
4. a) They did not want to be forced into future wars.

◆ Fan-N-Pick/Showdown (pp. 175–176)

Page 175
1. Allied Powers and Central Powers
2. France, Russia, and Britain (The United States joined later.)
3. Germany, Austria-Hungry, Turkey
4. Trench Warfare
5. Woodrow Wilson
6. Germany sent a telegram to Mexico promising help to get back US territory in exchange for help, Germany ordered submarines to attack US ships
7. April 6, 1917
8. November 11, 1918; Veteran's Day

Page 176
9. League of Nations
10. The Treaty of Versailles
11. They feared they would be forced into future wars.
12. Fourteen Points

United States Social Studies: Engaging Cooperative Learning Activities
Kagan Publishing • 800.933.2667 • www.KaganOnline.com

The Great Depression

◆ RallyCoach/Sage-N-Scribe (p. 186)

Left Column

1. a) Banks were careless with loans as people could not pay loans back.
2. a) Prices of foods and goods increased.
3. a) The New Deal
4. c) To provid pay to the unemployed and elderly funded by taxes of employers and employees

Right Column

1. a) Stock Market Crash
2. b) Banks took ownership of farms to help recover their loss in loans given.
3. c) To promote overseas trades to offer Americans work
4. d) Over 3 million young men were employed to work in forests and natural resources on environmental projects.

World War II

◆ Find Someone Who (p. 196)

1. b) Adolf Hitler
4. a) Hitler sent troops into Poland.
7. d) Protestors protested the war resulting in lower sense of patriotism

2. c) Ethiopia
5. b) Hitler broke a pact and attacked the Soviet Union.
8. b) Japanese Americans on the West Coast were placed in relocation camps.

3. d) France
6. a) Bombing of Pearl Harbor
9. a) Dwight D. Eisenhower

◆ Fan-N-Pick/Showdown (p. 197)

1. Polish and Jewish citizens
3. Nazis
5. 6 million
7. United States, Soviet Union

2. Holocaust
4. Hitler wanted to create a generation of young Aryans who were physically fit and totally obedient
6. Jumped from Nazi trains, escaped from concentration camps
8. United Nations

National Symbols

◆ RallyCoach/Sage-N-Scribe (pp. 213–214)

Page 213

Left Column

1. New York Harbor
2. To check for diseases, make sure the immigrants were healthy enough for work
3. Instrument used by inspectors to check immigrant's eyes for disease
4. Considered a risk to the public health
5. 2 weeks, or 14 days

Right Column

1. January 1, 1892
2. Statue of Liberty
3. 2%
4. Translators were provided
5. Various: famine or hunger in home country, religious or political freedom, educational opportunities

(Continued)

United States Social Studies: Engaging Cooperative Learning Activities
Kagan Publishing • 800.933.2667 • www.KaganOnline.com

241

U.S. Social Studies
Answer Key

National Symbols *(Continued)*

◆ RallyCoach/Sage-N-Scribe (pp. 213–214) *(Continued)*

Page 214

Left Column
1. Answers will vary
2. Answers will vary
3. Answers will vary

Right Column
1. Answers will vary
2. Answers will vary
3. Answers will vary

◆ Fan-N-Pick/Showdown (pp. 215–217)

Page 215

1. Loyalty
3. Francis Bellamy
5. Columbus Day
7. The "Flag of the United States of America"
9. Unable to be broken

2. No
4. *Youth's Companion*
6. U.S. Flag Code
8. Stand, face flag, right hand on heart, remove hat
10. Object that stands for something else

Page 216

1. Revolutionary War
3. Closed the windows, locked the doors, and posted guards
5. States would lose too much power
7. To explain the freedoms of the people
9. December 15, 1791

2. A special meeting in Philadelphia to plan a better government
4. George Washington
6. Senate
8. June 21, 1788
10. Delaware

Page 217

1. 50 stars
3. School, post office, town square, baseball games
5. "Don't Tread on Me"
7. Wrote "The Star-Spangled Banner"
9. Attack on World Trade Center, 9/11

2. 13 stripes
4. Revolutionary War
6. 13 original colonies
8. 50 states
10. President William Howard Taft

United States Social Studies: Engaging Cooperative Learning Activities
Kagan Publishing • 800.933.2667 • www.KaganOnline.com

United States Social Studies: Engaging Cooperative Learning Activities
Kagan Publishing • 800.933.2667 • www.KaganOnline.com

243

United States Social Studies: Engaging Cooperative Learning Activities
Kagan Publishing • 800.933.2667 • www.KaganOnline.com

United States Social Studies: Engaging Cooperative Learning Activities
Kagan Publishing • 800.933.2667 • www.KaganOnline.com

245

United States Social Studies: Engaging Cooperative Learning Activities
Kagan Publishing • 800.933.2667 • www.KaganOnline.com

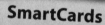